MISBEHAVIN' A TO Z

When Behavior Becomes Misbehavior

Carol M. Hoffman, EdD

BALBOA.
PRESS

A DIVISION OF HAY HOUSE

Balboa Press books may be ordered through booksellers or by contacting:

Balboa Press
A Division of Hay House
1663 Liberty Drive
Bloomington, IN 47403
www.balboapress.com
1 (877) 407-4847

Because of the dynamic nature of the Internet, any web addresses or links contained in this book may have changed since publication and may no longer be valid. The views expressed in this work are solely those of the author and do not necessarily reflect the views of the publisher, and the publisher hereby disclaims any responsibility for them.

The author of this book does not dispense medical advice or prescribe the use of any technique as a form of treatment for physical, emotional, or medical problems without the advice of a physician, either directly or indirectly. The intent of the author is only to offer information of a general nature to help you in your quest for emotional and spiritual well-being. In the event you use any of the information in this book for yourself, which is your constitutional right, the author and the publisher assume no responsibility for your actions.

Any people depicted in stock imagery provided by Thinkstock are models, and such images are being used for illustrative purposes only.
Certain stock imagery © Thinkstock.

Print information available on the last page.

ISBN: 978-1-5043-8818-4 (sc)
ISBN: 978-1-5043-8820-7 (hc)
ISBN: 978-1-5043-8819-1 (e)

Library of Congress Control Number: 2017914491

Balboa Press rev. date: 09/26/2017

FOR
JACKSON

**AND HIS ADORING FAMILY
IN ALPHABETICAL ORDER**

**AUNT CINDY
AUNT PAM
AUNT TRACY
DADDY
GRAMMY
GRANDMA
MIMI
MOMMY
PAPPY
UNCLE CARMEN
POP POP
UNCLE CHUCK
UNCLE JOSE
UNCLE TED
UNCLE TOD**

INTRODUCTION

The Introduction will give you an idea of what the book is about. Following the brief Introduction is a second kind of introduction called, "The Beginning." There is misbehavior in each "situational" true story. You'll find humor in some and sadness in others. There is no age limit to misbehavior so I wanted you to meet young as well as older folks. You'll find the entire book written in an informal style – no formal chapters, no footnotes, no bibliography, no words you can't pronounce or understand. There are four sections in the book – after the first section called "The Beginning," the second and largest is called, "Misbehavin' A to Z." The third is called "Beyond A to Z " and the fourth and final section is called "No End to Misbehavin' Yet."

I believe behavior is never accidental - which means good behavior is not accidental just as misbehavior is not accidental. We behave with a purpose or goal in mind – we choose what kind of behavior will get us what we want. Then we go after it in either positive ways or negative ways.

The biggest challenge for me was to develop an A to Z concept – an attempt to explore a word for each letter of the alphabet with each word having meaning to all the other letters. On some writing days, I thought I'd lose my mind.

This is my 8th published book. All are non-fiction, and influenced by the work of the late Alfred Adler. I know I write with my heart and then with my words. Sometimes it works and sometimes it doesn't work as well as I hoped. For sure, I believe what I write about. Those beliefs were transformed and developed into educational programs and projects for more than 30 years. I'm still at it, although this is probably my last book.

I like to think the concepts, ideas and suggestions within these pages can be useful to the general reader, although much of the exploration focuses on today's public schools and family dynamics. People were born to live their lives in a social setting. Like it or not, we must learn to get along with one another. Misbehavior has no age limit. If you have a lively, alive and spunky 80 year old mom or mother-in-law, you can bet she uses misbehavior to get her way.

My main reason for giving birth to a book like this is to shine a spotlight on the frightening increase in serious misbehavior – in our homes, our schools, our entertainment, our professional athletes, on our highways and in our communities. That spotlight is aimed frequently toward public schools and their developmentally inappropriate curriculum and standardized testing that have no place in the elementary grades. The "one size fits all" curriculum, K-12, does not work these days – maybe it didn't do a great job in the past, although daily life at home, at school and at work were more structured and less complicated. Consider this. Today's kids are still kids – it still takes 9 months for a full-term birth. They all begin to walk and talk around one year of age. They like to play with family and friends. They like ice cream and sand boxes, although not both at the same time. Their brain development still takes the same amount of years to reach a fully closed fontanel. They enter kindergarten pretty happy to be there.

But wait! That's yesterday's news. More brain-damaged babies are being born and developing more slowly than babies born in my baby days. Between fetal drug and alcohol damage as well as damage from a mother who smokes, poor nutrition from birth on, family in disarray, poverty, physical and sexual abuse and more, it's childrens' **situations** that are different and more complex than they were for children of the past. They have the same basic needs of children of the past although they also have different and special needs. Intervention programs are essential as well as costly. And so, the one-size-fits-all public education system just doesn't work anymore.

The overuse of computers worries me in that the kids aren't going to learn how to develop and deal face-to-face with others who are both alike and different from them. The addictive quality to electronics worries me. So, too, is the suspicion that the brain of today's children is being wired differently. Is that good or bad? When will we find out? General misbehavior bothers me a lot – misbehavior beyond school and home and into the community, the playground and workforce. Lots of misbehavin'going on. Kids and family are my life. Maybe the concepts, stories and ideas throughout will be useful to others who also care about kids and family. All stories are true. All names in stories have been changed.

My own children were my best teachers about kids. They are adults now yet remain my precious kids, always. Actually they are "our" kids – my husband's and my precious kids. Special thanks to Jill for being my editor.

THE BEGINNING

She yells at the top of her lungs. "Jeremy, get down here this minute!" Silence from upstairs. She tries again. "Jeremy, must I call you again? Get down here this minute!" More silence from upstairs. "Jeremy Louis Jenkins!!! Get the hell down here. Must I call you again? I won't do it. Won't call you again." Another minute of silence prevails.

"Jeremy, no supper for you tonight if you don't get down here right now! I even got the DeGiorgno pepperoni pizza – the kind you like. The expensive kind! Get down here right now before it burns."

She finally hears a voice coming from upstairs – definitely not Jeremy Louis Jenkins' voice. It's her daughter's voice telling her that Jeremy is on his computer playing an important game.

The loving mother that she is, she collapses on the bottom step of the stairs and starts to cry.

I am 12 and fairly new to the community. We recently moved from a housing project and now live in a small town outside the city. We are renting a large apartment. I am walking on the sidewalk along our street, doing some errands for my mom when I see three older boys heading my way. I feel kind of tense, although as they get closer, I recognize the big boy in the middle as a neighbor. He is about 14 and his name is Russell. He really is huge! And, if my eyes are working properly, Russell is actually carrying the other boys on his back. Both are smaller than Russell but look a few years older.

I know I'm not seeing things. I'm a bit scared yet I have to keep moving forward. Can't run away. As I am about ten feet away, I lose my fear and timidity and shout, "Russell! Why are you carrying those boys?" I could tell that he was straining terribly to keep from falling. His face was sweaty and red and he was breathing heavily.

The two boys told Russell to stop before they reached me. They said, "Blimp! Blimp! Stop!" They slid off his back and approached me. They asked me, "What's your problem, Girlie?" I said I thought that what they were making Russell do was wrong. I said they could hurt him. Both boys laughed in my face. Then they turned to Russell and demanded he tell me to "get lost." Russell yelled, "Get lost, girlie." The boys said he had to say it louder. He obeyed. Finally, the boys said, "Let's go, Blimp!"

I was fighting tears. The boys had blocked my way so I couldn't continue walking unless I crossed the busy street or turned around to run home. I decided I couldn't do either. I just stood there and glared at those awful boys. As they turned back toward Russell, they laughed like hyenas and climbed on his back. Their hands were clasped around his neck and shoulders. They weren't yet ready to move on. I waited silently.

The smaller of the boys demanded that Russell tell me how happy they made him. Russell said in a raspy voice, "They make me happy." Then the bigger boy whispered in Russell's ear. Russell turned back to look at me and said, "They do fun things to me."

With that, the huge boy labored on with those two bullies on his back and I hurried ahead. I was so shook-up, I knew I didn't want to go into the store like that. All I wanted to do was go home to my mom and tell her why I couldn't finish her errands. I waited at an intersection until I felt safe enough to turn around and go back home. And that's what I did.

That was only the second time in my life that I felt serious anger and fury for human beings. The first time was when I found out a year earlier about the extent of torture my mother's stepmother inflicted on her. For some reason, I've carried the Russell situation and my mother's abusive stepmother in my mind all my life. The remembrances bother me today – after all those years.

Luci was in the bedroom, turning down the duvet when her husband came through the doorway all excited and happy.

"You what?" she yelled at her husband.

"I bought a new truck. And keep your voice down. The kids are sleeping." Eric shifted from foot to foot, obviously agitated.

"Oh, you drop the news that you bought a new truck and expect me to be happy about it?"

"Come on now, Luci. Don't act like you didn't know I was looking at trucks for a coupla weeks now."

"A couple of weeks? More like a couple of days. And weren't you looking at used trucks?"

"Yeah, but when I saw the perfect truck for us..........."

"No! You saw the perfect truck for YOU!"

"Keep your voice down. The kids will hear us arguing."

"As if we don't argue every day!"

"Let's not go there, Honey."

"What's the difference in cost between a new truck and a used truck?

"It depends," Eric murmurs.

"Yeah, it depends if the guy buying a used truck uses his brains instead of his butt." Luci is really getting into this argument.

"Cut out the low blows, Luci." He laughs at his witty comment which does nothing but add fuel to the fire.

"How much did this 'perfect' truck cost?"

Eric thinks for a few seconds before saying, "Honey, it's not about what it cost. It's about what we saved. We got the best possible price reduction. Couldn't resist it. Plus a seven year warranty."

"Don't you dare 'Honey' me. And don't give me that weak argument about a seven-year warranty and the line of crap some salesman gave you about lowering the price. We can't afford a new truck! Our credit cards are already maxed out. Soon we'll be in the poor house."

"Oh Baby," hubby says in his best soothing voice. "I didn't charge the truck on my credit card. Duh. You know I couldn't have done that if I wanted to."

"Well then, how are YOU going to pay for this perfect new truck? Huh? Huh! Tell me that."

"Uh, well, uh. Sweetheart, I took out a loan at the dealership – with that new bank on River Street."

"And?" Luci barks.

"And........and.......and we'll have a loan we can handle just fine."

"I hope you didn't put my name on the loan."

Twenty seconds pass in eerie silence. Eric says nothing. Luci will have to launch her final salvo.

"You didn't!! Tell me you didn't co-sign for me. That's illegal."

"No but, honey, we must go to the bank first thing in the morning – as soon as the kids get on the school bus. After we sign, I'll even treat you to an I-HOP pancake breakfast. Won't that be fun?"

Luci walks over to their bed. She snatches the pillow from Eric's side and says, very quietly, so the sleeping children don't wake up. "Find another place to sleep. At least until the loan is paid off."

The phone rings ten times before Buddy's Grandma answers. At 82, she is careful with her movements. The voice at the other end says it's her great-grandson, Buddy. "Hi Grandma," he says.

"Buddy? Is that you? You sound different."

"Yes, it's me. I have a cold. Say, I'm a little short of cash and I could really use a loan from you."

"But Buddy, aren't you still in college? Didn't I pay all of that for you? I sent you spending money, too. Remember that five-hundred dollar check I just sent a few days ago?"

"Sure, Grandma. But I had to use it for the...uh, for the...dentist. I had to have my ...my...what are they called? My wisdom teeth pulled. Cost two thousand dollars and I had to put that five-hundred dollar check you sent as a down payment. You can see I still need fifteen hundred as soon as you can send it."

"Buddy – must I send another check?"

"Could you wire it instead?"

"Wire it? Wire money? What's that nonsense?"

"Oh sorry, Grandma. That's just another name college kids gave to checks. A check will be great."

"Okay. Should I send it to the same place?"

"Yeah. Send it to the same college. But I moved to a different dorm – you know – a different room in that building. Put my new roommate's name on the check. He goes to the bank for me when I have too much studying. Got a pen and paper handy?"

"You know me. I am like the Energizer Bunny. Always ready to take messages when the phone rings."

"Good for you, Grandma." He tells her his new roommate's name and then spells it for her.

She does what he asks and reads it back to him. He then gives her his new dorm address and she reads it back to him.

"Grandma, when does your mail guy come?"

"Girl. My mailman is a girl."

Buddy laughs. "Grandma, you have a great sense of humor. I love you."

The 82 year old voice says, "I love you, too."

Just another day. Just another scam. The real Buddy will soon find out. The fake Buddy finds himself in a lot of trouble. Grandma gets her money back.

Cassandra is a 7th grader. She is one of the smartest students in her class. She is also the biggest attention-getter the principal, Mr. Tanaka, has ever seen. She will not respond to anyone who calls her Cassie. Twice her school attire was so off-base, Mr. Tanaka had to send her home for an appropriate outfit. Just when the principal thought he had convinced Cassandra that it doesn't pay to break school dress rules, he gets a call from her homeroom teacher, telling him Cassandra is wearing an inappropriate T-shirt. Mr. Tanaka says, "I'm on my way."

When the principal saw the message on the back of her T-shirt, he had to stifle a laugh – after all, his sense of humor had to stay hidden. The back of the Tee said, "FART IF YOU HATE SCHOOL."

The principal put on his disgusted face and told Cassandra she either had to call her mother to bring an appropriate shirt to school for her or she had to go into the girl's bathroom and turn it inside out. Cassandra thought for a second or two – then pointed in the direction of the girl's room and headed for it. Mr. Tanaka just shook his head as he read those words on the back of her shirt. He could only imagine how disruptive things got for the homeroom teacher when some of the kids in the classroom began to respond to the message. He marveled at Cassandra's brains and wit, although he couldn't just ignore her antics – her joyful misbehavior.

A minute later, Cassandra backed out from the bathroom. She turned her back to her principal to show him that she obeyed. Then she waved bye to Mr. Tanaka, made a left turn down the hall. Luckily, the principal didn't quickly turn around to make a right turn. He suspected what Cassandra had done. She had not turned her shirt inside-out. Instead, she had reversed the back to the front. The forbidden letters were still there for all to read. He almost ran to catch up with her.

"CASSANDRA! CASSANDRA! My office. NOW!"

BEHAVIN' AND MISBEHAVIN'
A TO Z

A

ATTENTION

Attention is one of the most important needs and wants of human beings. Those needs and wants last a lifetime. When children and adults seem to get enough positive attention in their daily lives, they are seen by others as "good kids" and "wonderful neighbors" and "active, loving old people who still do volunteer work and go dancing."

We often call attention-seeking children an itch we can't scratch. On the other hand, for reasons that seem logical, children attention-seekers are more appealing to us than adult attention-seekers who we tend to call a pain in the butt.

Children who feel they don't get enough positive attention will learn a pattern of behavior that is annoying – mostly what we'd say clowning around, making noises, chewing gum and blowing bubbles that pop with just the right volume. The misbehavior is not serious, and the misbehavior stops for awhile – until the next time. In schools, most students who clown around but don't overdo it are actually liked by the teachers and classmates. They are attention-seekers we can live with. They don't physically hurt others. What's more, we see many of them on TV. They are our comedians!

Kids who do not receive positive attention at home find that negative behavior can get them attention when they push smaller kids off the swing or yell, kick or stick a pin in someone's balloon. Negative attention is better than no attention at all for attention-starved children. Attention-seeking behavior is the mildest, less serious form of misbehavior, although that behavior is annoying – it ticks us off and temporarily requires our response. Attention-seekers will annoy us, for sure. They will interrupt us just when it's the last thing we want them to do. And our patience will be tried, time and again. In school, the first name of the most attention-seeking student will be heard frequently throughout the school day. Remember Cassandra? She's a good example of an attention-seeker. How do you think she behaves at home? How do you think her parents cope with her antics, pranks and jokes? It's doubtful her parents find everything she does easy to overlook. It's more likely they wish their daughter would display behavior that could be described as positive and acceptable.

Getting attention in positive ways tells us we are worthy of notice – that we feel we have an important place with others – that we actually matter to those in our family and those in school and those in the community.

I belong!
I fit with people I want to fit with!
I never want to feel like I'm on the outside, looking in!

As for how adults can best respond to those who are wearing them out with annoyances, whining, yelling and arguing, try ignoring as much of the misbehavior as possible. If that isn't an option, assign a logical consequence. In general, the best time to give attention-seekers positive attention is when they are *not* seeking it! Teachers are pretty successful at reducing negative behavior. Most attention-seekers will never totally give up that behavior. Sometimes, reducing unwanted behavior is the best we can do.

We've begun our travel with the letter A. There are 25 more letters to visit. Let's make sure we inject some humor and minor mischief here and there. Before we get to the letter B, you need to have some clues – to avoid feeling overwhelmed by 25 more topics. Just keep in mind that each of the remaining 25 letters are related, intertwined and connected to Attention. It all begins with A. Many practical ideas will be offered – in plain language. Once we're through the alphabet, roll up your sleeves and be ready to try out new ideas.

FYI. Attention will soon merge with three other letters of the alphabet to form a concept that further explains behavior and misbehavior. This concept is easy to understand and is called The Four Goals of Misbehavior. Rooted in common sense, each Goal will be explored. Attention happens to be Goal 1 of the Four Goals. Things will become clearer as we move along in alphabetical order.

For now, let us **B**

B

BUT

There's a little humor with BUT so please humor me. Sorry if I sometimes stray from the seriousness of a topic and offend someone. A heavy topic needs a little lightness now and then.

Adults communicate far too often in conversations with one another – family, friends, co-workers – in ways that can mess up a relationship. They tend to be totally unaware that the way they sometimes speak to others is not helping the relationship. Until a good observer catches them mis-using their BUT and mentions it to them, they'll likely find themselves either angering or hurting others' feelings into the future.

Here is an actual conversation overheard a few years ago.

Vera comes down the stairs wearing a new outfit. Charlie is drinking coffee in the kitchen. He acknowledges her with a nod and goes back to reading the sports page. Vera makes a 360 turn in front of him and then says, " I didn't hear the wolf whistle when I came down the stairs." Charlie finally looks up from the newspaper and says, "Didn't I? Oh, sorry." – and returns to his paper. Vera is getting impatient. She comes right out and asks him what he thinks of her new outfit. Charlie finally awakens to his dilemma. He says, "Oh, I thought you wore that to Sharon's wedding – when was that? About ten years ago?"

Vera explodes, then calms down. Charlie attempts to vindicate himself, smiles and says, "It's nice **BUT** you looked thinner in the dress you wore to Sharon's wedding."

Charlie showed his BUT and Vera left the room in a huff. No more conversations between them that day.

Charlie is like many of us who show their BUT fairly often. We don't realize that once the word BUT is said right after a compliment, the one who just got butted only hears the words that come *after* the but. The compliment at the beginning of the sentence is forgotten.

Here's a situation shared by a mother who learned to reduce her But.

A mother of two children – a girl and a boy. – loves her kids and gives them lots of healthy attention. The girl is 7 and the boy is 5. Both have daily chores to do. The chores are appropriate to the interests and ages of the kids. The mother's one negative issue is that she shows her BUT too much. On a typical Saturday – when most chores are required of both kids, she notices her daughter has completed all but one of her "jobs." She says, "Way to go Katie. Snoopy knows his food is coming soon."

As she sees her son heading for the TV, she shouts, "Cameron Lee Jones!" as her son seeks his channel. "You made your bed and way to go BUT you didn't put your socks in the hamper and you didn't hang up your good jacket and you didn't feed the cat and now you have your hands on the remote, probably trying to watch a channel I don't want you to watch!"

Mom storms out of the room in a bad mood, leaving her son to turn off the TV and his sister to giggle at his discomfort. Cameron turns to face his older sister. He asks, "How come Mom always calls me Cameron Lee Jones when she's mad at me? She never calls you Katie Marie Jones?"

Mom's But opened up another issue - the Favorite Child syndrome. Lots of luck with that hornet's nest. For sure my husband and I loved and cared for and about all three of our children. There was no favoritism. Jill was the first born, so she was our favorite first child. Ted was the first-born of the twins and also our second child – so he was our favorite second child. Tod was the second-born twin and also our third child, which made Tod our favorite third child.

How could they argue with that? Well, sometimes they did.

Still, they grew up to be perfect adults.

For now, O SAY CAN YOU C?

C

CARING

Caring is a word that means different things to different people. For example, if you are caring for a sick child, you are the caregiver. If your aging mother is caring for her grandchildren while their mother is working, your mother is the caregiver. Sometimes she's even called the care*taker*. Why? Because she always tells her friends she is "taking care" of her grandchildren.

The word Caring is so essential to human growth and development and a healthy mind and body, it's hard to know where to begin. So let's begin here.

Love and Caring do not mean the same thing – at least to me. My strong belief my whole adult life is that Caring is more important than Loving. Of course, the capacity to love and receive love are important throughout our lives. Still, some people give love to others who take advantage of them – to others who take love without returning it. That's misbehavior. Pretending to love another yet faking it is misbehavior.

Bess was taken advantage of. She sings mournfully about it in a song from the 1934 George Gershwin opera, *Porgie and Bess*. Twenty-five years later, it was made into a popular movie. In the movie, Bess suggests maybe she really ought to quit "Lovin' Dat Man Of Mine." She knows her love for him is on a one-way street.

Love can be turned on and off throughout our lives. Caring, however, needs to go on forever. It must.

Caring is connected with Attention – our first alphabet letter just two doors back at A.

Caring is first felt in sensory ways by an infant as he receives attention from his mother, father or someone else who truly cares about him. Although the infant won't "remember" this early caring, he will be influenced by the sensory benefit of that caring. He feels good about it. It calms him, it warms him, it nourishes him, it gives him comfort whenever he needs it. By the time that well-cared-for infant reaches about three years of age, he is on his way to creating a happier adult life than those babies who never received the constant, appropriate caring of ideal caregivers. Caring and Loving join together very early in the hearts of parents and grandparents and others in a baby's and toddler's beginnings. Those are the most fortunate children.

In summing up two concepts that should be easy to explain, I realize I may have complicated things. Here goes again.

The best argument I have to offer to my belief that Caring is more important than Loving is this: Caring is more of a DOING thing. LOVE is more of a FEELINGS thing. What's more, how many people can you actually love in your life? You know – true and lasting love? Four? Ten? Thirty?

On the other hand, how many people can you actually Care for and about in your life? I want to say ALL OF THEM! We <u>can</u> care for people we know but don't really love. How often has a neighbor or co-worker or relative gone through a bad patch in her life? You might not love her – heck, you might not even like her that much - but surely you can care about her well-being.

When interviewing teacher candidates, we made sure we asked each one this question: "If you are hired for this position, will you love all your students?" Wow. You should have seen how they almost lost their composure, shifting in their seat, figuring out how to respond, fearful of saying, "yes" and also fearful of saying, "no."

You may think that's not a fair question of a potential Rookie teacher. Oh, but it is. It's not only fair, it tells a great deal about a person's ability to handle hardballs in his/her daily work with kids – and ultimately, their parents. Today's teachers often see themselves as entering a combat zone when they cross the threshold of their classroom.

To clarify that question about loving all their students, we don't let the candidate continue to wrestle too long in silence before responding. We say something like, "We're not looking for you to answer that question with a "yes." You see, we believe it's not realistic to ask our teachers to love all their students but rather that they care about them. In fact, we want all our teachers to care for and about every kid in their class."

The relief on the Rookie's face is priceless to behold.

Caring is the birth of Empathy.

Some really smart influential people have even suggested that without early sensory and caring-loving in the first year of a child's life, he may never develop empathy. If that doesn't scare the devil out of us, I don't know what will. What are the consequences of a young child not receiving the right kind of caring and love from the adults in her life? Here is my response:

MANY OF THEM ARE EITHER IN PRISONS OR IN GRAVES. OTHERS ARE IN YOUR SCHOOLS AND NEIGHBORHOODS.

Too harsh? No, too true. Far, far too many of this nation's children are entering school as damaged goods. If they were neither loved nor cared about at home, why would we expect them to enter the front door of the school as anything but damaged goods?

Care about those kids. Care about them every day. Never give up believing you can make a positive difference. And never give up on a damaged child's individual capacity to strive and thrive – to transcend life at home with new and positive possibilities for a better future – during the school day.

Early childhood teachers can make the biggest impact on children who enter school damaged in physical, emotional and social ways. This is not to say teachers of older students cannot make a positive impact. They can. And in so many school districts, they do. One way will be explored when we reach the letter **J**.

For now, however, we move along to the letter D

D

DOLLARS

Wanna get rich? People tell us to play the Lottery. Or at least scratch cards. Some people play on a regular Friday after-work basis. They advise us to "Keep away from those two dollar ones. They're all losers."

I'm told by several people that they only buy $20 cards. "Those are your best chance for a winner."

While standing in line to get a fuel receipt, I ask the person in front of me who is buying a $20 card, "How many twenty-dollar cards do you buy over a week's time?" She kind of cocks her head – as if she was thinking about the question – then scratches her head (she's good at scratching – you know – from scratching so many Lottery tickets).

Finally, she tells me, "Oh, only one twenty-dollar card. Plus three five- dollar cards and............um.............two one- dollar cards." My own mastery of arithmetic tells me this person spends $37 dollars a week on scratch cards.

I'm shocked! This woman is pregnant with her second child. (The toddler who is grabbing candy bars from the shelves is her first-born).

$$$$ are very important to human beings on what is likely a global basis. Americans don't have to travel to exotic islands or go on a cruise any more to gamble for $$$$. All they have to do now is hop in their car or on a casino bus that will take them to the nearest casino. Like Walmarts and a variety of Dollar stores, Casinos seem

11

to be getting nearer and nearer to home. Soon there will be one in your neighborhood.

Now I'm not knocking people's love affair with casinos and scratch tickets and major Lottery tickets – only last week I bought three $3 dollar scratch cards at the local fuel station – one for my husband, one for our son and one for me. Did we win? Well, our son and I won nothing except the rising hope of a winner – only to be crushed by the loss of $6.00 and a vow to never buy another scratch card. Maybe my son's and my total loss was because we used a penny to scratch. Do you think it might help if we had used a nickel or a dime to scratch?

As for my husband's card, it turned out to be a free card. What kind of gambling is that? It turns out his free card won another free card which, when scratched, won nothing but silver dust on top of the kitchen counter.

What does gambling have to do with behavior or misbehavior? Lots. Gambling is about money and money issues appear to be a big reason people fight, hurt each other and divorce. Money issues can hurt other relationships – like friendships – and cause them to break apart. By now money issues could have surpassed sex issues as the #1 reason marriages and relationships end. It makes no sense to me how sex could drop to second place, especially with all those Viagra commercials seen 40 times a day on TV.

To be fair to the gambling industry, marriages and other relationships fail for reasons other than gambling and sex. Other reasons – and there are many of them - tend to be spending money on things they don't need with money they don't have. In other words, using credit cards that are NOT paid off by the end of the month. Paying high – almost obscene interest rates - on those credit cards without the cash to back up purchases is a common behavior which is really misbehavior.

Two well-known money - tips gurus are Dave Ramsey and Michelle Singletary. Dave is the fellow on TV who used to show his audience novel and creative ways to get rid of their credit cards – forcing those people to come up with a monthly budget they can handle without ever using a credit card. Michelle, on the other hand, writes a syndicated column in major newspapers on managing your money. Like Dave Ramsey, she also offers courses for married couples – or other couples – to help individuals in a long-term relationship to become better handlers of money. They both have great ideas. Those ideas are certainly helpful to people who are bad managers of money – or people who need help developing a monthly budget.

Money may not truly be the root of all evil. Just some. After all, we need money in order to live our daily lives – first making sure our needs are met before moving in the direction of buying wants.

Making a Needs and Wants list is simple for a couple or even a single person to make. All you need is a few pieces of paper with holes punched in the paper. Place the hole-punched papers in a binder and get to work creating a monthly budget.

Now comes the hard part.

Under your Needs list, write every expense you'll be having each month – things that are somewhat "fixed" expenses like the electric bill and the car payment. Bills like car insurance that arrive on a six-month basis need to be divided by 6 in order to get the correct monthly amount. Bills that arrive on a 12-month basis need to be divided by 12 in order to get the correct monthly amount. You probably don't have to be reminded of this but (there's the but word) I'll remind you anyway. Once you feel confident you have listed all those fixed expenses, write the monthly cost next to each item and add them up. Now compare your monthly Needs cost with your monthly net income. Be honest! Do not use your gross income to fool yourself into believing you can cover all your listed Needs with gross income! You're smarter than that. Remember, we all have deductibles from our paycheck.

Let's finish up on Needs. If one of your Needs is for restaurant visits four times a week, reduce those visits until your net income increases. Eat your meals at home more often. Dave Ramsey reminds us that eating beans and rice several times a week won't kill us. A family of four can eat at home for less than $2.50 a person. How? Open a family size can of the soup of your choice (ours is tomato), crush those out-of-date Ritz or Saltine crackers into the soup for increased intake, add Doritos to the meal with Salsa, of course. Eat all of it for $2.50 per person. Drink water and actually save the cost of a $2.39 soda for each person had you eaten in a restaurant. The soda alone, that you didn't buy, saved you $9.56. Don't forget you saved fuel cost for having to drive to a restaurant for your dinner. This proves that eating at home more often saves you big bucks. That cost-saving meal at home would even allow you to add ice cream for dessert. Of course, that means buying a half-gallon of store brand ice cream which is, sometimes, very tasty.

And please - understand this: Visiting restaurants four times a week is NOT a Need. It is a Want. Confusing Needs with Wants is deliberately misbehaving.

Offering 7-week parenting courses during those almost 30 years in public education at the two public school districts where I was fortunate enough to be employed was special. Occasionally, parents-to-be took the course. We always had a mixture of parents of preschoolers and parents of our district students, K-12th grade. Making lists of Needs and Wants was always a real eye-opener to those parents. We made a serious topic a lot of fun. Exploring Needs and Wants was one of the parents' favorites. They could easily grasp the fact that if they wanted to keep their marriage intact along with raising kids to be well-behaved and thrifty, they needed to control their own spending. They got this message: Dollars create misbehavior in families who do not live within their monthly budget.

Learning to be good parents and just plain good people throughout life requires a sufficient amount of dollars and an abundance of good sense and self-discipline.

The next letter is the first letter of a word that is another super important one to internalize. That word may be the most common one for creating relationship problems and break-ups. Let's look at Expectations.

Writing this book made me think hard about the double-meaning of the word expectations. For years, I didn't realize there are two different meanings to that single word. The one you are about to meet are expectations that can mess up relationships. The other kind of expectations you'll come to later are about teacher's and parent's expectation of children's behavior through following rules, completing chores and general good behavior.

The letter E – for Expectations

E

EXPECTATIONS

Expectations is a word – when activated within a family or among friends – is so powerful, it can cause ruptures in relationships without anyone ever realizing what happened. More often than we can fathom, the bad effects with Expectations hit us almost every day. Maybe even every day! The weird part about it is that its negative effects can be so swift coming at us that we think to ourselves, "Where did that come from?" Many people never figure out the real reason. Once we truly know the reason, we can do something positive about it..

There are two types of expectations. The type we'll be exploring with our **E** word is different from the type of expectations we'll be exploring later with the **P** word as well as other places where we discuss school rules and consequences. In those places, expectations of students in a school setting are essential. For now, let's look at problems with expectations in families.

Here's another true story. Names and some locations have been altered to protect privacy.

The Rodriguez parents have been giving their 12 year old son, Ben, a weekly allowance for two years. He's generally a good kid and contributes throughout the week by feeding the pets and washing his father's car. His allowance started when he was 10. He got an increase when he was 11, going from $8 a week to $10. Now that he is 12, he expects an increase to $14 or $15. He is already several weeks into his 12ᵗʰ year of life without a word from his parents that his allowance is overdue.

Instead of asking his parents, "What gives here? No pay? No raise in pay?" he becomes moody and sometimes surly. The past two weeks he's more sarcastic than usual with his sister and he gives the dog less attention.

His parents assume it's just a stage he's going through.

One day, Ben decided he couldn't hold it in any longer. At the dinner table, after his sister, Staci, asked if she could buy new shoes for a big dance at school, Ben shouted, "No way! She's always asking for money and I don't even get a crappy allowance. Maybe no two-dollar increase either."

The 15 second silence at the dinner table was broken by Ben's mother. "Ben, Staci's not getting new shoes even though she wants them." Then looking at her, their mother said, " We'll work something else out. I know how to dye shoes. Let's give that a try."

Staci finishes her dinner in silence and then excuses herself and goes to her room.

Ben's Dad clears his throat and questions Ben about his attitude. "What the heck was that all about after your sister asked for shoes?"

Ben told his Dad he was PO-d because he didn't get a raise this year. He didn't even get his old allowance two weeks ago. All his friends already get more allowance. He embellishes. "Chip's Dad gives him $20 a week. Barry's Step-Dad gives him $25. And what do I get? A crappy ten bucks. I'm not in elementary school anymore, Dad. It's not fair."

Grappling with his anger, Ben's Dad calms down before he says, "Know what else isn't fair? In order to keep my job, I had to agree to a twenty-five dollar a week cut. My cut started two weeks ago."

The silence in the dining room was deafening.

Finally, Dad broke the silence with a quiet few words. "Take notice. You did not get a cut. Just me. You'll get your $10 weekly allowance beginning next week."

Jake tells his experience with expectations "gone nuts." They are told in his own words.

"My grandmother is basically an okay person. Kind of cool for an old lady. It's just like here of late she's getting really demanding of my mom – who just happens to be my grandma's daughter. I'm 19 and live at home with my parents. I'm going to the local Community College, which means I can bum off my mom and dad for meals and a free room. That's how I know almost everything going on around here. And what's going on around here is one unhappy mom and one unhappy grandma. It used to be more fun around here.

What's the problem, you ask? Here's my two cents' worth – just because I'm a computer science major doesn't mean I can't smell a big stink coming from those two women in my family. Here's how I figured it out.

Before my mom got a job where she gets paid, she was what you'd call a ....whatchamacallit.... a housewife. She took my grandma for groceries every Tuesday. Mom would treat grandma for lunch and then go grocery shopping. Then take grandma to her apartment, unload all the stuff from the store – and then Mom would come home and start supper for Dad and me. Oh yeah - and for herself, of course. By the way, Mom's a really good cook.

Well, ever since Mom started her job – which is parttime, - grandma has been miserable. Mom works on Monday, Tuesday and Wednesday at our doctor's office. Already you get the picture, don't you? Tuesday? Can't haul grandma around on Tuesdays. Guess who is v-e-r-y unhappy? Uh huh. Grandma. Grandma plans her whole life around Tuesdays. Tuesdays are the only days Grandma wants to go to lunch and grocery shopping. Grocery shopping is now on Fridays with only enough time for a fast-food place for lunch 'cause Mom has too much else to do on Fridays after working three days a week. Mom's not coping well with the new plan either, 'cause all grandma does is complain and bitch and bitch and complain. Mom's getting very tired of it all and threatens to buy ear plugs so she can cope with Fridays.

And guess who else isn't coping very well with Mom's work schedule? You guessed it. My Dad! He complains about the kinds of suppers

Mom makes on Mondays, Tuesdays and Wednesdays. To give Dad a little credit, though, he doesn't complain as bad as grandma. He even apologizes after Mom reminds him how much extra money she is making for our family. So Dad's getting used to hot dogs on Monday, Pizza on Tuesday and Mac 'n Cheese on Wednesday. Me? Well, I'm perfectly happy with those meals. Besides, I get them for free."

This 19 year old son is pretty smart in a number of ways. I'll let the reader figure out the number of ways he is smart. For our exploration of the letter **E**, however, the above is a prime example of what happens when Expectations suddenly undergo a major change.

Grandma wants what she has had for years. Lunch and grocery shopping on Tuesdays with her daughter. She could count on Tuesdays for a long time and she isn't about to roll over and love the change in her weekly schedule. She hates lunch on Fridays at either Burger King or Taco Bell. And she hates the sauces and sour cream they put on their food. And where's the fine linen and waitresses and waiters looking lovely or handsome who always gave grandma extra-attention every Tuesday – like clockwork? (Notice how our **A** word sneaked in here?}

Grandma also hates shopping for groceries on a Friday. It's too crowded on Fridays. The carts are hard to find. People are rude in the aisles. The shelves aren't stocked fully on Fridays. And on and on.

The 19 year old son added, *"Grandma is being selfish. She doesn't appreciate my mom. I don't know how mom can take it much longer. This Saturday, she said she thinks she's getting hives from it all. She even hinted that maybe she should just quit work and go back to Tuesday shopping with grandma.*

When she said that at lunchtime on Saturday, Dad and I almost choked on our stir fry and pieces of steak. We knew the cheesecake would follow. So we both yelled, 'NO, NO, NO, NO, NO!!!!!'

Seems like Dad loves the extra income. As for me, keep the hot dogs, pizza and Mac 'N Cheese coming."

Expectations. Sometimes they can almost ruin a happy family.

On the other hand, expectations are looked at differently in a school setting. Rules and consequences developed by teachers, principals and students are made for expectations in a social setting – like schools – or Scouting programs, Summer Day Camp, Day Care, and others. Once rules are made, agreed upon and enforced, students are expected to follow them. No excuses. This different kind of expectation is explored in other areas of the book.

Ben could not win this round with expectations. It was also looking like he wouldn't be getting an increase in allowance anytime soon. Maybe not even that piddling $10 that was already two week's late. His expectations were not met. He was also left with feelings of guilt. Disappointment first, then embarrassment, then guilty feelings because his Dad was hurting and hadn't told him about his job problem.

Jake's story is a different one. It's almost self-explanatory, so let's be brief with the exploration.

Teenagers like Jake universally consider their grandparents "old." He assumes that it's Grandma's being old that turns her into a real whiner and complainer who doesn't appreciate all the stuff his mom does for her. He wonders why Friday lunch and shopping has to be any different from Tuesday lunch and shopping. What's the big deal?

It may be true that many older folks have expectations that are never to be reduced, changed or, God forbid, cancelled! Just try it and you'll see. The results can sometimes be akin to a nuclear attack or a tornado. Jake is learning a lot about expectations – but he probably doesn't really "get it" yet. Sometimes people go through their entire life without realizing that many of their relationship problems rest on the letter **E**.

Expectations! On to the letter **F**

F

FAIRNESS

Fairness tends to be a word people use as a protest. Sometimes to express disappointment and almost always as a way of letting others know they didn't get what they expected.

There's that expectation word again – we just left it and are back to it already.

In a way, expectation and fairness are married – or at least kissing cousins. While they are almost alike in meaning, they really aren't identical. Let's go back to Jake's grandma's disappointment in having to give up her beloved Tuesday lunch and shopping trip.

To grandma, having to move from a Tuesday event to a Friday event wasn't fair. Why wasn't it fair? Because it didn't meet her expectations! Grandma wanted what she expected. When she didn't get what she expected, she cried, "It's not fair!"

How did Grandma's behavior – really *mis*behavior – affect her daughter's own feelings? Ironically, her daughter's feelings were almost identical to her mother's. So were her words. The daughter said, "After all I've done for my mother, you'd think she would be grateful – learn to accept a change in my life that meant a different lunch and shopping day in hers. She didn't lose our get-together, just a change in the day of the week! It's not fair!"

The daughter – Jake's mother – had fully expected *her* mother to accept a day-of-the-week change with good humor and gratitude. Ha! Not!

Expectations. Fairness. Yes, they are almost married to each other. Lots of divorces occur because of the relationship between expectations and fairness. There's lots of misbehavior going on in human beings of all ages. It's not just old folks like me who expect life to be fair when we forget to remember that ancient axiom. We know the axiom that speaks the truth. We just don't want to accept it.

LIFE IS NOT FAIR.

Here is another way of looking at the F – word: **Fairness**.

One of my professors at Temple University – Dr. W – spent more than an hour describing and explaining the difference between Equality and Equity. His exploration was fascinating. Dr. W first looked at Equality by defining it in two words: THE SAME. Then he defined Equity in three words: SIMILAR YET DIFFERENT. He sure knew how to get a person's brain to shift into a higher gear!

The sameness of equality and the differentness of equity became another road to travel on the road to understanding human behavior and human relationships. Sometimes we want the same as someone else. When we can't or don't get the same – and it's really, really important to us that we have it – our thoughts and sometimes spoken words are: IT'S NOT FAIR!

Another example of equal/equity issues frequently come up in families during the reading of a deceased person's Will. Let's say old Max dies and leaves a Will. In his Will, "50% of all my withholdings, possessions and property go to my brother, Robert, and 50% go to my brother Sammy." Robert and Sammy would appear to receive exactly the same thing from their dead brother, Max. That would be truly equal.

Oh, really?

The appearance of 50/50 equality is not necessarily true equality. It would be pure equality if Max liquidated his property and possessions and came up with a monetary value instead of "stuff." If the total value of Max's "stuff"was $200,500 and that sum was divided equally, both Robert and Sammy would receive true equality – all in cold cash.

Another variable in Max's Will had to do with equality vs equity yet nothing to do with monetary inheritance. Perhaps Sammy was the brother closest emotionally to Max. Perhaps Sammy took care of Max for a year before Max died. Perhaps Sammy paid many of Max's doctor and medical bills. On the other hand, Robert may have visited Max just once during Max's long illness. If these things really did happen that way, Sammy could be disbelieving and angry about the Will to the point where he lets the lawyer and his brother, Robert, hear these words, "It's not fair!"

Sammy didn't mind that Max was trying to be "equally" generous to his brothers, but he said he wished Max had divided up his estate in a more fair way. For example, 75% to Sammy and 25% to Robert.

Notice that this kind of distribution wouldn't have been what had seemed equal. Instead, it would have been equitable, at least in Sammy's mind. He was adding value to all the ways he cared for and about Max during Max's illness. On the other hand, Robert, the brother receiving 25%, might have been satisfied with receiving less. We'll never know.

There's a whole lot we'll never know about the true and actual relationships between and among people.

The above example might have been shorter in explanation. I just didn't know how to do it. A complicated topic like equality vs equity is hard to simplify. The example, however, is common and creates many hurt feelings and anger after the Will is read. Equality and Equity need a great deal of thought when deciding who gets what in YOUR Will – in advance of your death, of course. In the above example, hard feelings, long-lasting resentment and outright estrangement occurs because the "giver"- who is now dead - didn't understand how essential it was to make sure the final Will does not create long-term relationship problems between those mentioned in the Will. Some lawyers comment that Wills create more misbehavior among siblings and other relatives and friends than anything else.

Equal means absolutely the same. As a result, equality is much more difficult to achieve then equity.

The history of equality, discrimination and civil rights haunts us yet today. How and when will there be understanding, compromise and caring for all? True 100% equality may be impossible to achieve in social, economic and cultural areas of people's lives – at least any time soon.

There may be no need to further explore the really complex issues that come out of the equality/equity interpretation. It does matter, however, to realize how human relationships tend to rupture when not enough thought is given to the way we treat others in our lives. A great deal of misbehavior can occur when one person wants to be treated equally with another in a specific situation and then at other times, treated in equitable ways.

Here are a few quick examples. They are kind of silly, yet they make the equal/equity problem perfectly clear.

Equality will not exist when one child in a family needs braces to correct an over-bite and the others do not.

Equality will not exist when the mother in a family does all the cooking, cleaning, child-rearing, laundry and out-door work along with a job outside the home and the father does not.

Later we'll look at some ideas to help children and adults avoid the misery of falling head-first into the pit where someone yells, "It's not fair!"

Gee, we're already at G

G

GLOCCAMORA

With the letter G, we'll be concentrating on the skill of "Doing the Unexpected." It's best to try it out a couple of times with minor misbehavior from others – even your pets - unless your only pets are in a fishbowl. Evaluate the results and sharpen your technique until you become good at it. The most important first step in developing this skill is getting good at remembering what you typically say or do when in conflict – words and actions that not only do not solve anything but sometimes escalate things. When you sense you are about to enter a blow-up situation, Doing the Unexpected can be effective in stopping the blow-up in its tracks.

Whenever the other person is doing something you don't like or saying something that irritates you - STOP before you leap! Take 5 seconds of silence to come up with a reply or action *different* from the one the other is expecting. Let's call those 5 seconds the "Pause that Refreshes." One example: When our children were ages 14, 11 and 11, I began my first teaching job. I liked to say it was my first time "out of the house" since our three children were born. I was a stay-at-home mom. My husband and I made that decision before our first child was born. He took on three jobs and I took on three jobs plus - at home.

My husband and kids were great about taking on more chores and fewer homemade cakes and pies when I entered the world of teaching. They were even interested in talking about my adorable students. They also helped me prepare some projects and gave me good ideas for activities.

So where was the fly in the ointment? My mother-in-law.

Remember Jake's grandma? The grandma who made the family miserable when her day out with her daughter was moved from Tuesdays to Fridays? Well, my mother-in-law behaved in a similar way.

When I began teaching, I did not phone my husband's mother as often as I had in past years. I also did not go shopping with her or visit her as often as I used to. The result? There were many phone messages from her when I would get home from school. As a first-year teacher, there was a whole lot for me to learn – and I stayed after school longer than other teachers and arrived at school in the morning earlier than they did. That meant I not only didn't take (or have) the time to phone or do things with my mother-in-law, I also didn't take (or have) the time to return all her phone calls.

How can you both love a mother-in-law and feel really angry with her at the same time? Well, I could. Resentment was building in me and I was upset that she couldn't understand how busy my life had become. I didn't want to begin a shouting match with her that could hurt our close relationship and start WWIII. I was expecting her to be happy that I had reached my goal.

An idea came to me while driving home - I had recently taken a psychology course with an emphasis on the impressive work of Alfred Adler and Rudolf Dreikers. They referred to their work as Individual Psychology or the Psychology of Use. A simple yet powerful body of knowledge and skills. A common sense approach. Practical. Easy to learn and use.

And so, when I got home that day, exhausted at 5 PM with kids to chat with the minute I walked in the door – guess what happened? Yes. The phone was ringing off the hook. The kids told me that Grandma keeps calling and hanging up on them when they answer. They were confused. She loves them. What's going on?

I took a deep breath, threw my purse on the floor and dialed the number I hadn't dialed often enough since school began. She answered on the 3rd ring. I said a friendly hello and she said, in a really nasty voice, "I thought you died!" Uh oh. Might as well get this over with. Try to do the unexpected. Just try it. "Hm," I said. Then I took a deep breath.

If I had said what I really wanted to say – "So you want me dead, do you? How could you be so cruel and selfish? Sorry to disappoint you. I'm not dead!" – my next move would have been to slam the phone down and disconnect her. So instead, I took that 5 second pause and said in a calm and caring voice, "You miss me."

There was an unnatural silence from my loquacious mother-in-law and then there was sputtering at the other end. I waited until my mother-in-law almost whispered, "Well...well... yes. You don't call me anymore. You don't answer my calls. We don't go to lunch."

I needed another 5 second pause. Might as well try the unexpected one more time. I quietly said, "I'm a bad daughter-in-law."

BINGO!!! For the following several minutes, my mother-in-law began defending me until I thought she was going to recommend me for sainthood.

Finally I interrupted her accolades. "You really miss me. I'm sorry I couldn't phone you as much as I used to. Let's come up with a plan that will work for both of us. Not now, though. I'm late getting home and the kids and I have dinner to get ready. Is that okay with you?"

It was.

The next evening we made a plan over the phone. I agreed to things I felt I could handle and she gave up expecting daily calls from me as well as lunches during the school year. We continued to love one another. Doing the unexpected became one of my favorite ways of dealing with misbehavior from that day on – no matter what the age of the one misbehavin.'

Gwen and her husband were in one of my parenting classes. Gwen was the mother of two daughters, one age 12 and the other, age 11. Her focus was consistently on the misbehavior of 12 year old, Tara. One evening, Gwen shared some of Tara's antics with others taking the course. She also shared the things she said every time Tara misbehaved. The way Gwen responded just wasn't working. Yelling and screaming prevailed every time.

Most of Tara's misbehavior was arguing with her younger sister, Mikala, calling her sister names, accusing her sister of taking Tara's combs, brushes, and pens. On and on – the same old annoyances and anger.

I asked if Gwen was ready to try Doing the Unexpected. She said she was ready! And so we explored several ideas, finally agreeing on something. Gwen is Irish and friends tell me she has a powerful singing voice so I asked if she knew the song Glocca Mora. She knew of it but would Google it to make sure she knew all the words.

We decided on a plan. Gwen's husband agreed to support his wife. The other parents in the class cheered her on and could hardly wait for next week's class - unless there was no misbehavior from Tara. Gwen and her husband had a really good laugh about that. They both guaranteed there would be something to report next time.

The plan went like this. Next time Tara ran to Gwen to tattle on Mikala, Gwen would stop, stand up straight, shout "Show Time," and belt out the song, Glocca Mora. The next time happened two days later. When Gwen stopped and yelled, "Show Time!" both girls stopped in their tracks. As Gwen belted out the first verse of Glocca Mora, both girls were stunned and silent. And by the time she reached the second verse, both girls turned and ran upstairs.

Gwen had just given her daughters notice that she was no longer getting involved in their petty misbehavior. Did that end the sibling arguing? Gwen reported that she only had to sing Glocca Mora one more time. Since Gwen's husband was in on the plan, he even joined in singing along. Both daughters again put their hands over their ears and ran upstairs.

I saw Gwen a year later at a school event and asked her how Glocca Mora was coming along. She laughed and said that now all she has to do when she sees tattling or an argument coming is to start humming it.

Does this mean Gwen and her husband are pleased with their daughter's good behavior every single day? Of course not. Kids don't give up ALL their misbehavior – even when they fly the nest. If parents and other adults choose to learn how to defuse a misbehaving person by a silent count to 5, they'll have time to think instead of react. Thinking instead of reacting is impossible in an emotional state. Think! Then act! Don't react! The other person always wins when we do that.

There is no magic to "Doing the Unexpected" or "The 5 Second Pause" or other ideas we'll be sharing. They just work and are all based on Common Sense. There are other ideas and techniques to learn and unleash on others who are misbehaving.

First, however, we need to finish the A to Z Alphabet. Get ready to be happy.

Here's **H**

H

HAPPINESS

Happiness is overrated sometimes, mostly because we expect it for 16 waking hours – along with 8 hours of happy dreaming. Another expectation shot to . . . . you-know-where.

Ask 10 parents what they want most for their children and all – or almost all – will say they want them to be happy.

Ask 10 teenagers what they want most in life and all – or almost all - will say they want to be rich, especially rich and famous.

I've done this kind of questioning eons of times with the same results.

If parents want happiness for their children and if teenagers want big money and fame most of all, what does that suggest? Can money buy happiness or can happiness make you monetarily rich and famous?

Are happy people called winners? Are rich people called winners? Most seem to believe that winning makes us happy and losing makes us unhappy. Winning gains attention, trophies, blue ribbons, and fame that may also bring them $$$$. Not winning trophies and ribbons makes people unhappy except for those blessed few who compete just for fun. "Winning" a 2nd or 3rd place ribbon makes some people unhappy. I have seen evidence that this behavior (MISbehavior) is increasing on Field Days and at 4th of July foot races and other track and field events. The predicted winners don't always win first place. When an unknown speedy kid comes along and wins the Blue Ribbon by two feet, the predicted winner often shows poor sportsmanship – aka, misbehavior. Second-place ribbons have been found on the grass after an event. There's no happiness there for the expected winner except for those kids who have learned they can't always be a first-place winner in all challenging areas of their lives.

When taking a course that focused on life as we want it and life as we actually live it, a college professor defined life this way. *Life is a series of adjustments.* Just six words – six words that say a lot. Then he mentioned "the pursuit of happiness." One person in the class thought she had caught the prof in an error and called him out, "No, that isn't the way it is. Our Constitution *guarantees* happiness for all its people." After a 5-second pause that kept him from sarcasm, the prof joyfully said, "No way! Go look it up in the Constitution. The Constitution allows us to *pursue* happiness. There's no guarantee." Not giving up, the student smiled as if she caught a Prof in an error. (Some people don't know when to stop.) Then in a superior voice, she said, "Well, aren't unreliable rights the same as a guarantee?"

Unreliable? And she's going to be a school teacher?

How many young adults in this country assume they are guaranteed happiness under the Constitution? How many school students know exactly what the Constitution is – and how it was developed?

No person will be happy every moment and every day of his or her life.

If our wants from birth to death are to "just to be happy," and "also to be rich" we'll end up in the unhappy bin at an early age. We must expect to encounter many adjustments throughout our lives – adjustments for good things but mostly adjustments for the bad things that come along. We need to become really good at meeting those inevitable life adjustments head on with courage and a pinch of good humor.

Folks who suddenly become rich overnight upon winning a BIG LOTTERY may find the adjustment very difficult. Becoming wealthy *instantly* requires people who are in shock and disbelief for days and weeks to make instant decisions about the rest of their life. Gaining or earning money over time may be the better way to accumulate wealth that you can enjoy as you move through life. Getting rich quick appears to bring more problems than the winners could ever have predicted.

That reminds me of a big, burly dad in a parenting class whose response to my belief that instant wealth from a big Lottery win can be a bad thing. He stood up, folded his hands in a prayer-like way, looked up to the ceiling and begged, "But at least give me a chance!" Needless to say, we all laughed.

More than anything else, the individual person is the one who truly makes his or her happiness. Happiness starts from within. We have to stop counting on happiness to come from lotteries, scratch cards and horse races.

Now is a good time to introduce you to a man who is helping elementary and middle school students gain happiness from within. Sometimes students can gain happiness by losing. By losing, at times, this special person is teaching his students how to eventually gain happiness as winners. And he is doing it all through the knowledge and skills of chess.

Dr. Jeff Bulington of Memphis, TN accepted the challenge of traveling to Franklin County, MS – a small and very poor county with a population of about 7,000 – to work with school children. For some wonderful and caring reason, an anonymous benefactor would pay Jeff Bulington's salary if he takes on this project. He agreed. He left a more affluent area in order to teach Franklin County's low income 5th and 6th graders how to become winners by mastering chess. Before Dr. B arrived, these students had been almost guaranteed an adult future of $8.00 an hour jobs – that's if they could even find a job. And then an amazing thing happened when Dr. B came to town. He brought students the possibility of developing internal happiness – happiness that would spread beyond chess, and bring great happiness to the town's population.

The CBS program, *60 Minutes*, recently highlighted what happened to poor, low-functioning school kids with country-style grammar and little hope. When Dr. B came to town, in one year, he transformed them into successful chess players. Yes! In one year! Once the kids learned to play chess, their grades improved in academic subjects. Behavior became impressive. Parents were amazed and happy. Attitude and self-esteem soared.

At one point during this first year of learning to play chess, a state-wide competition was scheduled. Dr. B asked if students were interested in entering this competition. They were, although Dr. B warned them that they would likely lose their matches because the others competing had years of practice and were top-notch. He prepared them to handle the likelihood of losing all their matches. He touched on how they would feel, emotionally and socially. If/When they did not win their matches, they would shake hands with their competitors, smile and politely thank them for the match.

As expected, the Franklin County students did not win. Dr. B would not accept their apologies for losing. Instead, he said he was glad they lost! The kids were shocked at his response. He told them that a person who loses a match learns more than a person who wins.

Indeed, Dr. B's words were prophetic. In the next scheduled state-wide chess competition, Franklin County won! And no one in the county became rich in money. Instead, proud students and their parents and teachers achieved a happiness they never experienced before. In addition to teaching chess to elementary students (now including kindergartners!), Dr. B also demonstrates humility and applies little value to trophies for winning. Skills and accomplishment are a child's own best prize.

There's much happiness in Franklin County, MS these days, ever since Dr. Jeff Bulington came to town. He's my newest hero.

Google Dr. B and make yourself feel happy.

Before we move on to the letter I, let me say, I wish you much true happiness in your life.

I's have it

I

INFLUENCE

Searching several dictionaries for their definitions of *influence*, I came upon a surprising number of variations. What was most surprising was Webster's New World. Here's what I found: *Power to affect others; Power to produce effects because of wealth, position, ability.* What I found via Google seemed more in tune with our journey – *The capacity to have an effect on the character, development or behavior of someone or something.*

The capacity to have an effect on the character, development or behavior of someone or something.

Influence goes both ways. There is good influence and there is bad influence. Good influence helps with character development and is best begun the first three to five years of life with parents and family who are loving and caring. And so we want the parents of every child born to have a good or positive influence on their young child – parents who see a child as a blessing. Those early years are the foundation years and they set a behavior pattern in motion that will likely take the child through life.

Years ago, psychologists and others who studied human behavior were able to examine the unwanted behavior of a child or adult and discover why by using those two words:

CAUSE and EFFECT

These learned men and women always knew what the effect was. That was the easy part. Most of the time "effect" was behaviors like biting people, using a baseball bat on someone's head, stealing purses, stealing cars, killing someone – and on and on. The cause, however, was usually the same:

His childhood is to blame.

Almost always that is true. Early influences are so important – still, every child is different from every other child. Even identical twins don't behave the same in every situation. And brothers and sisters born of the same mother and father tend to show differences as well as similarities in personality and behavior patterns.

That's why the common conclusion, **His childhood is to blame**, is far too general and vague and wide and deep and diverse to pack into a single cause. Causes are difficult to distill down to a single one. In days of yore, it might have been much easier to use the term cause. These days, we realize that many, many factors of family, school, economic status, personality, wants, needs, use of drugs and alcohol, gang membership and social life impact on a child's behavior over time. All of them together could be causes. The list could be endless. And so, for our purposes, we prefer to use the term *influence* instead of the term *cause.*

INFLUENCE AND EFFECT

This is a good place to reveal the name of my favorite NBA player - Stephen Curry of the Golden State Warriors. A recent interview by Tim Kawakami of *The Mercury News* found Steph describing the influence his father has had on his life. Steph's Dad – a stand-out player of his own generation named Del Curry – helped his son accept receiving less salary than 81 other NBA players – and be happy about it. Being one of the top 3 NBA players and not misbehaving about being paid considerably less than those lower performing players is amazing. While he is making a hefty 12.1 million dollars this year, it means 81 other players are being paid even more! It's uplifting that the NBA star doesn't see his lower salary anything to complain about. Here are Stephen's words during the interview. "One thing my Pops always told me is you never count another man's money. It's what you've got and how you take care of it. And if I'm complaining about forty-four million over four years, then I've got other issues in my life."

At age 29, Steph Curry seems to have his priorities and values well-established. He still looks about 14 as he did when my husband and I watched him play for the Davidson Wildcats. Along with his wife and daughters, his parents can take a bow. Their awesome influence on their son gives us all hope that other professional athletes will follow his behavioral path. (Note: Today's newspapers revealed Curry will be paid $40 million a year for the next several years. His patience and attitude paid off big time!)

Professional athletes are a major influence on our nation's children, both positive and negative. Curry is one example of a positive influence on children. There are many more examples. Unfortunately, televised games show us frequent images of baseball players who strike out and then take their bat and destroy it, as if the bat was to blame for their inability to hit the ball. Last week, a player who struck out slammed his bat across the top of his leg and repeatedly attempted to break the bat in half. Finally the bat broke in half and he stormed to the dugout. He's probably on the Disabled List for self-destruction of his leg. A few weeks ago, an MLB player took his bat to a waste can until he destroyed it. Last week, several pitchers deliberately hit opposition players at-bat and injured them. Some had to leave the game. Last night, I saw a pitcher angry with an umpire's call go into the dugout and take a bat to any available item other than a human being. Why do Major League Baseball players misbehave like that? Because they believe they lost control and have to "get even" with some past or present - real or imagined -event. They call this a "pay back." Where are the consequences for this kind of malicious misbehavior? Why do managers accept this kind of misbehavior? What do these vivid images do to millions of kids watching in person or on TV? They are not images that influence kids in positive ways. It's akin to that other out-of-control behavior known as Road Rage. The only way to end misbehavior in professional sports is to apply logical consequences immediately, along with a hefty fine and at least one day's suspension. It should be ended because a few are hurting the image of the majority. The vast majority are mature enough to handle stress, disappointment and the short end of the final score. There's always another game to play – and win.

If I were writing during football or basketball season, there would be more examples of bad behavior. The MLB season just happens to be at the forefront of my favorite TV viewing – Channel 659 on the Root Channel. Go Bucs!

Sometimes we choose the people we want to influence us. Where we "fit" in birth order has an influence we may not even be aware of. My brother is 8 years older than I and was my greatest influence in my love for sports. Siblings can have a life-long influence on the directions we end up going. Having a grandparent living in your family as you were growing up has an influence on you and your siblings. The death of a parent while you are still a child has a strong influence on you. As we mature, we make conscious or un-conscious decisions about good influence vs bad influence. A child around the age of two is now a purposeful decision-maker, although that may be hard to believe. What is the favorite word of a two-year old? No!! That's the time we want to begin steering the child in the direction of developing acceptable behavior. When that steering is not taking place in the home, children will continue to enter school with few, if any, appropriate social skills and self-discipline. Their behavior will be more unacceptable in a group or social and academic setting. And so the good influence of school teachers and day care staff is essential. They will be the ones expected to build a behavioral foundation that should have been already built by parents in the home.

Gang membership is another troublesome issue. Gang membership is increasing in cities and now moving into rural areas across the United States. The following is an excerpt of an eye-opening article written by a life-long resident of the small town of Danville, Virginia. The writer is Eddy Lloyd. His article was published in the *Chatham Star-Tribune* on June 7th, 2017.

"Gangs, in the simplest terms, substitute for relationships that are absent from the lives of the individuals. The gang provides the member with the sense of friendship, camaraderie, and family ties that are missing from home and school. It provides the member with successes that replace the failures experienced elsewhere."

Lloyd sees gang activities as a learned behavior. He goes on to write, "Parents or older siblings may introduce the activity to younger family members growing up in the household. This may explain part of the problem in Danville. The youth involved now are the kids of gang members. It's all they know. It's a shame to see 11-year olds get into the life but when they have nothing and gangs have something to offer, that's why they get in."

Lloyd ends his article by emphasizing that schools alone can't fix the gang problems and police alone can't fix them just as an economic approach alone can't fix them. He ends his well-written and important article by writing,

"Schools, communities, churches and police all need to get together. Most concerned citizens are tired of what's going on, but it will take the community to fix the problems. Citizens need to be willing to help the police solve the crimes that are taking place."

And so, we know it will take people who care, people with courage, people with clout, people who were elected by us to fix problems, police forces, school district leaders and churches, synagogues and other houses of worship to tackle these major problems. It may take ten or more years before we can make a measurable, positive difference yet if we don't start now, what kind of country will our children and grandchildren live in? We can't give up the attempt to make a U-turn toward real positive change.

Today's child care staff and school teachers at all grade levels are struggling with far too many students whose misbehavior is disruptive and just plain unacceptable. Yes, it's not fair. Yes, we will do it anyway and take our temporary resentment out at the gym, the Dairy Queen, the pizza place, swimming, hiking or gardening. After a good workout, we'll remind ourselves that this is a job parents and families didn't take care of at home. Our positive influence on those who didn't get enough can and will make a difference.

Who influenced you in positive ways growing up? Are you "passing on" those positive influences to others?

On to the letter **J**

J

JEALOUSY

There are Seven Deadly Sins – I read about them years ago. I need a refresher. Is jealously one of them? Let's find out.

The first Deadly Sin is Pride. (no need to define it; we know what it means) The second is Avarice, which means *Greed for Money*

The third is Sloth, which means *Disinclination for work or laziness*

The fourth is Lust, *which means Pleasure; to feel an intense desire*

The fifth is Envy. (we know the definition of this one)

The sixth is Gluttony, which means *The habit or act of eating too much.*

The seventh is Ire which means *Anger or wrath*

Before we move on, I have to tell you that this was the most fun page for me to begin so far. It was fun to research the history, going back to 1000 AD. They were not truly identified as Seven Deadly Sins until somewhere between the 4th and 6th century. Sinning in a few of those seven deadly categories is a riot. My favorite is Gluttony. I never knew it was a sin to over-eat. Now I must admit, in print, that I sin almost every day. It just seemed to be a bad habit, not one that could burn you at the stake (oh, did someone just say "steak?" I'll be there in a minute) If Gluttony is a Deadly Sin, why haven't all those people walking around the Malls in tight clothes and inhabiting Pizza Parlors been arrested?

Sometimes it's hard for me to be serious. Sorry about that.

As we look at those Seven Deadly Sins in a list, let's talk about them in the language of human behavior.

PRIDE

AVARICE

SLOTH

LUST

ENVY

GLUTTONY

IRE

Where does our **J** word – **JEALOUSY** – fit on the list? Probably in more than one category. Jealousy and Envy are almost alike. Maybe Lust almost fits. How about Pride? If you are a woman who feels jealous of another woman's attractiveness or quality of clothing and her 10 pairs of Jimmy Choo shoes, is it because you "used" to look and dress like her and now you don't? Is your Pride injured? Could be, although Envy and Jealousy seem to be most alike.

Feeling jealous of another person is a common behavior in both women and men, although our culture tends to attribute that behavior mostly to women. Jealousy is not misbehavior unless it is acted upon. To <u>feel</u> jealous is just behavior. To *do* something hurtful or embarrassing to another is **mis**behavior.

Our schools and our workplaces are filled with **mis**behaving jealousy – the majority of it from girls and women. Social Media is often a haven for hurtful messages, hateful comments and unflattering photos. As an older woman, life-long sports fan and former tomboy, I choose to make these kinds of comments. When I look in the mirror, I see an old woman. Who is jealous of an old woman? School leaders and elected government officials in all Federal, State and Local positions must wake up to the frightening misbehavior of far too many students in public schools. Wake up to the stunning similarity of those ancient Seven Deadly Sins with the misbehavior among today's students. Jealousy may emerge at the very top of the list.

I'm wondering if our adult society really knows how deep, how wide and how problematic life is when the behavior called jealousy becomes **mis**behavior.

We ask ourselves, when and where does jealousy begin – that is, when and where do those feelings emerge and are then acted upon? In the crib? In the playpen? No, I don't believe so. In Day Care? Kindergarten? Maybe the seeds of jealousy are planted there. Elementary grades? Probably by 4th or 5th grade. High School? Yikes, yes! Big time sprouting of those misbehavior seeds.

Where does the influence of Family come in? It seems to me that we must be careful in laying all the blame or responsibility for misbehavin' kids on parents. In today's fast-moving technological world, once kids are in upper elementary grades, all kinds of electronics are, literally, at their fingertips. The computer and the internet and cell phone can take kids to places I've never been. In many cases, it takes them to places we don't want them to be.

Sure, parents should have guidelines, rules, restrictions and the courage and stamina to see that their kids follow them. The reality for many parents, however, is that their influence on their children's behavior greatly diminishes before their kids reach secondary education, especially in public schools. I-Phones, other kinds of gadgets, the internet, texting and other mind-boggling electronics are readily available for students to abuse. This abuse is leading to misbehavior far, far beyond soaping a neighbor's car windows or knocking on the front door at dark and running away before the old grouch opens the door – to find no one there.

One of my Dad's favorite examples of "olden days" misbehavior was to phone a tobacco store and ask the clerk if he has Prince Albert in a can. When the clerk says, "yes," the caller says, "Well, let him out!" and then hangs up.

I told that kind of misbehavior story to a class of high school seniors. Two laughed, most snickered and a few made comments like, "How lame." And then they all went back to sleep. (No, they didn't.)

Back to our **J** word. Once established, does jealousy never end? Most certainly it doesn't end in our colleges and workplaces – even in some homes. I'd guess it even continues throughout adulthood.

Where are parents in all of this during their childrens' early years? Certainly those preschool experiences play a major role in the way children begin comparing themselves to others. I believe the first three years of life are the most important in laying the foundation for a caring, loving, behaving human being who, as an adult, will not fall into the trap of misbehaving through jealousy – that instead, she or he will contribute in important and useful ways to their society. Where are parents during their childrens' middle and teen-age years? Do they guide and monitor their kids, set limits, say "ok" when they know they should say, "no?" Since electronics are an integral part of tweeners and teen-agers' every day life, will they learn to use their electronics appropriately and choose better roads to travel than becoming influenced by the negative effects of the internet? What part does jealousy play in their daily electronics experiences?

If we choose not to make serious positive changes in our children's and school students' way of life, we might have to add Electronics and Social Media to the list of The Seven Deadly Sins. By the way, the list of Seven Deadly Sins is not biblical, although religious figures developed them over many centuries.

Okay - On to **K**

K

KIDS

Children are my favorite people. All ages. Diverse family backgrounds. Poor, middle-class, well-to-do. Whatever their race and religion or lack-there-of may be, doesn't bias or influence me. All I care about is that they matter to others in their lives and are loved and cared for in their home. With the right beginning in life, those teens in handcuffs could be using both hands to carve wood or to paddle a kayak or to hug a toddler or to perform brain surgery.

Every child should be born a wanted child. However, even if a child was not planned, that child should still be born wanted the moment he arrives. The best start for a human being is to be wanted and cared for – and to also be loved unconditionally.

The first three to five years of age are, absolutely, the most important years of the life span of a human being. Once in public schools, we see more misbehavior in children whose family life is less than healthy. Single parents understandably tend to have a harder challenge with parenting than intact parents. Still, we see many single parents doing an admirable job with raising their kids. However, when all parents give their "all" to those first three years, their children have a better chance of functioning better academically, emotionally and socially. They also demonstrate good behavior.

Now let's look at older elementary and high school kids. How are they doing these days?

There's little use in citing statistics since studies and surveys differ greatly one from another. Data-gathering with teen-age populations in 50 states is like counting grains of sand in your hand just before the wind comes along and messes up your count. It's almost impossible. So maybe the best we can do is keep looking for examples of teens to admire and appreciate within our communities.

Between local newspapers and local TV stations, we can be pleased how many "thons," charity events and fund-raising activities are planned and carried out by teens in my part of the country. Our local channels frequently carry early-morning coverage of these kinds of admirable activities. The viewer can see with his or her own eyes that the teens they are viewing are really good kids! It's heart-warming and hopeful, until the "real" news takes over. Then we see extensive footage of a few teens and some in their early twenties in hand-cuffs, having been arrested for burglary, vandalism, assault, drugs, domestic abuse, rape, shootings, stabbings and murder. Putting more TV emphasis on a few teens in trouble diminishes the earlier and shorter coverage of many teens doing well in their communities. It's kind of like what can happen with your "but." Example: *There are plenty of good teens out there BUT the number of seriously troubled teenagers has increased significantly and the murder rate in our county is soaring, as well.*

National TV coverage also seems to move quickly from positive stories and images to negative stories and images. TV ratings supposedly go up with images of serious misbehavior and down with footage of good and heart-warming stories, activities and events planned and carried out by teens.

I'll borrow a line from our **F** letter. It's not fair!

For now, let's look at a different topic, perhaps one related to teenage misbehavior that doesn't seem to reach our newspapers and TV coverage. It's a topic that bothers me a great deal. Am I alone in this?

High School Dress Codes or None at All?

Question

What do high school students wear to the beach when they enter the school building dressed *for* the beach?

Here are some explorations of either a dress code or school uniforms for today's public school students across the country. One option is some type of uniform required to be worn in schools beginning in 4th or 5th grade – or begun at least by the secondary level and continuing through graduation from high school. Outfits should be attractive and trendy, yet modest. No skirts for females that look like the kind women wear on TV that appear to be painted on and are impossible to sit in for fear they'll ride up to their belly button. Clean jeans would be ok, too. Maybe jeans without holes in the knees deliberately put there by the designer or the person wearing them.

How about T-shirts that don't have lettering such as THIS PLACE SUCKS or GOT SOME WEED?

The school's "mascot" and/or the school's name could be printed on the Tees. Make sure room is left for breathing and expansion on the females' T- shirts. Colors could vary. Students could have some choices - two or three color options selected by a committee that includes the School Board, administrators and parents. Parent input has to matter to those who run the schools. We should all want our students' parents to partner with us.

For example, let's say the committee doesn't like the idea of T-shirts. If Tees aren't what the committee wants, how about front-button shirts? The only rule with front-button shirts for female and male students would be that the only button allowed to be **Un**buttoned is the top one.

For the males, chinos or jeans and polo-type or button-down shirts would work well.

No flip-flops for either gender, please. Not in school except on a few special days.

In warm climates of the country, shorts that reach just above the knee would be just fine for males and females. These days, many females - yet not all of them - enter the school building dressed for the beach. For some reason, male students tend to dress more appropriately for a place where very important academic learning is supposed to be going on for at least 180 days.

If some type of school uniform is not acceptable to a committee, develop a dress code that is strictly enforced. There is no dress code at all in some of our public schools. That just invites misbehavior! And in those public schools that have an established dress code, do administrators and teachers actually enforce it?

Much of in-school misbehavior beginning in upper elementary grades centers around jealousy - jealousy among students, mostly females, and most based on physical looks, clothing and possessions. I've even heard of Make-Up Wars among pre-adolescents in school. It involves who can come to school with the best make-up job. That's just nuts.

The arguments I hear which oppose a dress code for students beyond, say, 4th or 5th grade, holds no water. Opponents say it won't work anyway so why bother. How come it's working well in religious schools and some private, non-religious schools? And if cost is an issue, school districts can get their Purchasing Agent or Business Manager to find good deals that could greatly lower the cost for parents of students. Besides, money is spent on too many inappropriate outfits anyway.

How about Made in the USA?

Coming up with an effective dress code or required but trendy uniforms could take a year to develop. It may also take one school year of use to evaluate how effective the school's original choice really is. Should some adjustments need to be made, they can be made over the summer months and presented to the students, parents and community weeks before the new school year begins. Really, there's no excuse good enough not to develop and implement a dress code that can and will reduce student misbehavior, especially among secondary students. School is a social place that has too many secondary students taking hormonal and competitive advantage of the social, beach-wear, flip-flops freedom in far too many public schools.

If we can establish a well-implemented dress code in our public schools, I feel certain that up to one-half of our envy/jealousy misbehavior in high school will disappear. That will leave school administrators and teachers more time to deal with student misbehavior involving I-Phones, porno on computers, fights, and drug and alcohol usage, along with teaching academic subjects, of course.

From a J word, we've ended up exploring a major influence on student misbehavior - Jealousy – especially in the secondary grades. From there, we looked at Kids and Codes of Conduct as well as some type of school uniforms.

Lots to think about.

HERE COMES **L**

L

LIBRARIES

Yesterday, I read another article that predicted public libraries would soon be a thing of the past. A friend had also read that article. She asked, "Do you really think public libraries will just disappear?" My quick response was a strong, "No!" Then I gave the prediction some more thought. Maybe "Yes?"

Here in 2017, our public libraries have undergone some modernization over the past two decades. Before those changes began to take place, however, my view is that public libraries changed very little in towns and cities throughout the U.S. since the 1950s. I am familiar with public libraries in several states, although Pennsylvania libraries are most familiar to me. The library I frequent these days is the Degenstein Library in Sunbury, PA. It is located on the second floor of a huge building with more books than I've ever seen in a public library. So far, none of the paid and volunteer staff have spoken of a shortened future existence for public libraries. I can understand why. However, I have observed in my relatively new library the growing number of computers available to users. Other technologies are cropping up for users, as well. That makes many people in the community happy.

Still, something very important to book-lovers is not happening and it's not good news. Fewer people are browsing and borrowing the almost endless offering of books available. I do not exaggerate when I say "endless" because after 7 years of belonging to that library and borrowing books every three weeks, I have never gotten to half of the shelves filled with books. They still await me. I feel challenged to visit all of them.

Some days, I am mostly all alone among the books in this cavernous building, wondering where everybody went. Of course, I think I know where they went. They went to the other end of the building and settled at computers. I watch a few as they leave the computers. They head straight for the elevator and push the button for the first floor and home. They do not borrow books to take home for three weeks like I am doing.

After reading that article yesterday, I am feeling more troubled. Is the public library, as we know it, truly at risk? Are physical books gradually or quickly being replaced by e-books, U-tube and Google?

Marc Bodnick writes in a 2012 *Forbes* article about Tablets and eReaders, saying "… they are a much better way to get a book than borrowing it or buying it at a book store. You can get the book right away the split second you want it!"

Robinson Meyer of *The Atlantic* sees it differently in a 2016 article titled, "Fewer Americans are visiting local libraries and Technology isn't to blame."

Meyer cites the following as supporting his theory. A recent PEW survey found that just 44% of Americans say they use libraries or bookmobiles when a few years earlier a PEW survey found 53% were in that category. While the PEW people suggest the decline may be due to technology, the Institute of Museum and Library Services show years of less and less revenue from the year 2002 to the year 2013. Most likely both technology and reduced governmental funding are reasons for the reduction in book-borrowing in our public libraries. The combination of technology and money seems like the reason for the decline.

With so many smart people in this country, there have to be ways to rejuvenate our public libraries. There surely are ways to make our libraries a magnet for kids and adults alike. Creative thinking paired with dedicated volunteers and employees can certainly find ways to liven up public libraries. We can't let our libraries die.

Ben Franklin must be shaking in his grave by now. By the way, how many public school students know about Benjamin Franklin's role in "inventing" public libraries for the United States of America?

After searching for additional articles that suggest libraries are on a slippery slope, I go way back in time to my own first visits to my local public library. It is a story I have told often to parents, teachers and others. I'll tell it as if I am four years old and already in love with books.

My mom has been in love with books forever, so it is no surprise that I love books, too. The year is 1944 and I am getting closer to my 5th birthday. My Dad won't be home for my next birthday but he will be home for my 6th birthday – at least if the war is over by then.

My brother is eight years older than I am and he loves to read, too – mostly he reads magazines – mostly sports magazines and the sports page in the paper. He doesn't go with mom and me to the library at least two days of every week like we do. He's in Northwest Junior High School so he only visits our library during the summer. Anyway, when mom and I get ready to take our books back so we can get more books, we pack a bag for mom to carry and off we go. We have to walk about four or five blocks. We walk everywhere we have to go. I'm told we're poor because we live in a housing project. I never feel poor. My friends don't feel poor. Some people who don't live on the project but go to our church act like they're more important than us. It's not true though, so it doesn't bother me. Everybody else knows my mom is the most important person in the world. Everybody needs her for some kind of problem. The rich people even bring their dresses to be hemmed by my mom or their coat buttons to be sewed on. Mom never charges them anything but sometimes they give her twenty-five cents! People call my mom the project nurse even though she isn't a nurse. Others call her the shoulder to cry on – whatever that means.

Here we go, back to our walk to the library.

I love to take walks with my mom. She's my best friend. When we come to the bridge that crosses the Schuylkill River, she always takes my hand. She knows I'm afraid to cross the bridge – I'm always afraid the bridge will fall and we'll end up in the river. She never scolds me for being afraid. She just takes my hand and we both skip across as fast as we can. When we are safely across the bridge, we stop and get our breath back. Then we both laugh. Now we can see our library. I always get excited when I see it. All the books are waiting for us. We're just about there.

My only sad part of visiting the library is the librarian. I won't tell you her name because mom says it's not polite to criticize her. Maybe she's lonely, my mom tells me. Or unhappy. Maybe she doesn't have a family. Maybe she's tired from working hard. Maybe she just doesn't know how to talk to children. I think something but I don't say it. 'No, mom. She's just a nasty old maid.' I would get scolded if I said that so I just think it.

On this Tuesday, I decide to take out The Little Engine That Could. When I tell Miss Grouch I'd like to borrow that book on my mom's library card, she looks at me with those beady eyes and says, "No. You can't take that out again. You borrowed it last month. You borrowed it in December. You can't be selfish with that book. What if another little girl wants to borrow it?" Before I could "make a federal case of it" like my brother says about me, my mom says I should put The Little Engine That Could back on the shelf and find another book.

I wasn't happy about it but I did what my mom asked me to do.

As I was looking for a book I read a year ago, I decided to be brave and ask Miss Grump a question. My mom was busy in the adult area so she didn't hear what I asked until I had already asked it! Here was my question: "When can I get my own library card so I can take out two books instead of one on my mom's card?"

I could sense my mom freeze even though she was in another aisle. The librarian looked at me like I didn't have a bath for a week. I knew she didn't like me but I didn't care – at least that day. Miss G didn't say a word for a long time. Then she announced in that whiney voice, "No one gets a card in this library until he or she is in school. Are you in school?" She knew I wasn't. Still, I said I wasn't – that I would be five in six months. Miss G just sat there and stared at me. I didn't give up yet and finally asked if I could get a library card on my 5th birthday.

"Absolutely not!" she announced. "Besides, you would also have to write your name on the card – both first and last name." I was getting excited now. I told her that I <u>can</u> write my first and last name. I could see the wheels of crazy going around in her eyes. She was thinking. Quickly I asked her for a piece of paper so I could show her I could write my name. Reluctantly, she took scrap paper out of her wastebasket and slammed it on the counter. Then she seemed to calm down. I figure she didn't want my mom to hear her making noise. Miss G only allows people to whisper in HER library. Does she live here? Maybe. Anyway, she gave me a pencil and asked me to write my name for her. I printed my whole name neatly and with a growing excitement until Miss G almost smiled as she told me, "Sorry. You must write your name in cursive." My heart sank. My mom came to the desk and told Miss G we were ready to check out.

Mom was respectful and calm, as usual. She surprised me and asked Miss G, 'If she can write her name in cursive, could she get a library card before she enters kindergarten?' Mom smiled her most beautiful smile and waited as Miss G. sat there thinking. Miss G took the deepest breath I ever heard someone take. Then she said, 'Yes.'

On the way home I was so excited I forgot to be afraid of crossing the bridge over the Schuylkill River. As mom and I walked up the hill toward the project, I asked if she would teach me cursing. Mom laughed her best laugh without hurting my feelings. She explained that it's cursive, the kind of writing she writes to my Dad at her desk every night after I go to bed. 'It isn't cursing so don't worry about it.'

That night, mom taught me to write my name in cursive. After not even a half-hour, she said I was doing a good job. Then I asked if we could go to the library tomorrow instead of the day after tomorrow, like always. She smiled her YES so I knew I'd have my very own library card the next day.

And I did.

If you wonder what Miss Grump said when I wrote my name in cursive on the library card she handed me, it was a surprise. First, she smiled and said, 'I'll bet you had your mother up all night teaching you cursive.'

My response was, 'Oh no. It only took fifteen minutes on the clock. Then mom stayed awake all night writing to my Daddy.' Then Miss G smiled!

That day is a day I'll remember as long as I live. I checked out *The Little Engine That Could* and a second book. I don't remember the title of that book.

And so, all library-loving people will not allow their public libraries to shut down – not in our lifetime or our great-grandchildrens' lifetimes. With creative fund-raising, programs, projects and perseverance, libraries WILL survive. Let's reverse the odds together.

In the meantime, visit your local library and search for one or two really good books on misbehavior!

On to **M** which is also the **M**iddle of the alphabet

M

MEMORIES

"*Thanks for the Memories*" was a popular song sung by Bob Hope of movie and TV fame back in the day. Yes, I know. It's a song for old people. Still, it can be heard on the car radio every so often. Once you hear it, the song doesn't leave you for awhile – especially if your memory allows you to recall all the words. There was a later song that was popular called, "*Memories Are Made of This.*" That was a bouncy one and fun to sing. There are more examples of songs about memories but those two will serve our **M**'s purpose.

Memories are so personal to every human being on earth that it is impossible to exaggerate their importance. Have you ever considered how memories influence our everyday lives – how both good memories and bad memories guide us in making important choices, decisions and goals? The **I** word, **Influence**, fits perfectly with the **M** word, **Memories.** Our **A to Z** format purposely brings words, concepts and ideas together to make behavioral connections. The reader's memories are unique in that no one in the world has your bank of experiences and memories. Your memories cannot be replicated in somebody else's brain. Until science and technology learn how to transfer your unique memories to the brain of someone else, you are stuck and blessed with your own.

Why stuck? Why blessed? Let's look first at stuck. We have all filed away memories we wish we had not kept in our brain – the bad or sorrowful kind – and we wish we could just forget them. Some of us actually do allow our brain to forget some of those unhappy kinds of memories - yet all it can take is a life situation years later to trigger the brain to remember what you hoped you forgot.

You've read stories over the years about people who have "lost their memory" through some kind of trauma – a car accident, witnessing a murder, being hit on the head with a baseball or suffering a stroke are just a few examples. Sometimes that memory loss is permanent and sometimes it is temporary. I've interviewed several adults who wish the memories they lost in a terrible trauma had remained lost – but they returned anyway.

Memories, therefore, provide us with a mixed bag of what's stored in our brain throughout life. For now, let's focus on two ages of people. First, very young children and second, older folks who are probably retired or counting the days until they are.

Children between birth and about three years of age do not have memories as we know them. Parents who want to disagree tell us about their daughter's memory of a car trip to Montana at age 22 months when she counted a hundred elk and ate deer meat at a lodge made of stone and wood. What most likely happened is that the child – now older - is repeating what her parents told her years later about that car trip. And as that child adds more years to her life, she remembers and repeats what adults told her about it. During those first three years of life, the brain is not developed enough to process memory-making experiences. What I have learned over the years from countless early childhood specialists and neurologists is that most children cannot recall and describe any event or experience until they are four or five. All their earliest experiences are sensory – and they are very, very important. Seeing, Hearing, Smelling, Tasting and Touching. The five senses lay the early foundation for thinking, experiencing and making memories. To me, sensory learning is like the foundation of a house. You can't see it once it is in place because it gets covered up! Without a strong house foundation, the rest of the house is weakened and at risk. Doesn't the same thing apply to a human being?

By age four, five or six, the brain is ready to store actual memories and not just sensory bits and pieces from those first three years. Those true, stored childhood memories – those of the four and five year old - can be verified by their parents – and not invented by their parents. The child that age *can* store actual memories. To make this complex milestone clearer to understand, children in elementary grades and beyond are capable of storing and retrieving experiences they had when they were four, five or six. Some adults claim their earliest recollection was at age 7, 8, or 9. Everyone is different.

I'd like to add something I can't prove but believe just the same. I believe our prisons are filled with mostly young men who never received those vital, essential, "healthy" sensory experiences during the first three years of life. The main ingredients for "building" a good life depend on that sensory foundation. The seeds of developing good and acceptable behavior do not sprout in many home environments – sad to say. Misbehavior is learned early on and continues as a way of life for those kids beyond their early years. Misbehavior becomes a pattern for the emotional and social survival of children whose foundation is poorly established. Their bad behavior will almost force others to "see" them. They prefer seeking attention for bad behavior because they have become so good at it. It may sound awful to say, yet over the years I've come to almost admire the creative and non-lethal misbehavior of <u>some</u> survival-type children in school. Over time, they have developed a hard outer shell to protect their inner vulnerabilities and have learned well how to survive in a place where they know they don't belong. With a nurturing, caring and loving early childhood, those kids might have grown up to become the best and the brightest – and our world badly needs more of our best and brightest.

What are the childhood memories of these misbehavin' kids and young adults? We may never know. And if we could know, would we use them in positive ways to help misbehavin' teens and young adults decide to turn their lives around? We'll soon be exploring more about the health of our own memory and our memories called Early Recollections. We'll also be exploring The Four Goals of Misbehavior.

They will be better understood by the time we get to the final part of this book. When the Goals are understood and applied, they can and will defuse a potentially serious flare-up.

Older folks and their memories are a very different story from what we just explored with the younger folks. In many ways, people who retire fairly early find their next ten years among their happiest and healthiest - and with a brain full of remembrances. However, before some people reach their 70s, little health issues tend to crop up. When those health issues are physical issues like arthritis, eye problems, hearing loss, indigestion, frequent urination and other nuisances, family doctors can usually offer some help in the form of medication or physical therapy, a change in a person's diet – even a recommendation to see a specialist. On the other hand, when the problem with the older person is memory loss, that's another whole ballgame.

At first, memory loss may be seen as forgetfulness or diagnosed as Dementia. Sometimes dementia is seen in another as a struggle to remember almost all words and names that used to be easy for that person to say without a struggle. Others experiencing dementia may no longer function in the space around them. They get lost in their own space. Having a bit of a struggle with occasional words tends to be common in most older folks and not necessarily dementia. Sure, people doing an occasional grasp for that word or name they knew well all their lives is no fun, yet they realize it happens and they often laugh about it. When they are *aware* and can even make fun of forgetting a word or name, that's kind of good news. However, when the forgetting of common words and familiar names and places takes over and the older person doesn't seem to be upset about it – almost oblivious – then dementia may have become Alzheimer's – and that's not good news.

Why are we discussing Dementia and Alzheimer's in a book about misbehavior? Here's why. Being a paid caretaker or a non-paid family member of an older person whose memory is slipping beyond what others can "fix," creates problems for those caretakers. When the older person no longer realizes he has a serious memory issue to the point where he needs others to guide him everywhere and resolve all his social, physical, financial, bathroom and other important behavioral issues, he may be seen as a person who is misbehaving. If the caretaker believes the old man actually <u>can</u> follow directions and rules but chooses not to, verbal and physical confrontation may erupt. Newspaper articles and TV coverage indicate there is an increase in what they call "eldercare abuse." That's no surprise. Much of the eldercare abuse remains hidden or unreported. That's wrong yet understandable. It's wrong because our society is kept in the dark about the acute need for many thousands additional well-trained, caring and patient caretakers. It's understandable because caretaking is a very, very difficult job, especially when caring for old folks who can no longer meet their basic every-day needs. These old folks are not misbehaving.

Whether a caretaker for an Alzheimer patient is an unpaid relative or someone who is employed, the caretaker's work is one of the most difficult jobs we could ever imagine. A caretaker who is the daughter of an Alzheimer's victim told me she doesn't know how she gets through a four-hour shift without talking nasty or wanting to shake her father. She loves her Dad. It bothers her to have those feelings after a relatively short period of time with him. It's difficult for a caretaker to accept that the victim of serious memory loss can't still function at a higher level. It is at those times, an Alzheimer's victim is most vulnerable to physical abuse.

It seems to me that we can do the most good for memory-loss patients <u>and</u> their caretakers by reducing the caretaker's hours significantly and by providing a certain level of required training that will better prepare a caretaker for the role she or he is about to play.

We are living longer and longer in either good/OK health or poor/terrible health. The need for more and more well-qualified caretakers of the elderly could by now be acute. A favorite nurse was recently discussing this topic. Almost jokingly, she said that the biggest medical problem we have today is that people are living too long. She smiled but then became quiet as she realized she had revealed a truth this society and this country's leadership haven't quite grasped.

Or is it that our society and country leaders won't grasp, accept and do something about eldercare and caretakers until one of their own loved ones is affected?

The most vulnerable of us in this country happen to be our youngest and our oldest. The youngest have no retrievable memories and the oldest, have few, if any, retrievable memories. Think about it.

In the final section of the book, I will share with you my own experiences in occasional inability to recall a word or name. It's frustrating! In order to remedy this nuisance, I devised a way to help me when this occasional memory slip occurs. It only cost me 50 cents to "fix" my memory! More on that later.

In the meantime, while you're young-at-heart and fortunate enough to remember the words, sing along with Bob Hope. Thanks for the Memories.

On to **N** – the first letter of a sad word

N

NOBODY

Webster's New World Dictionary defines nobody as *no one; a person of no importance.*

I don't know how you feel about that definition – I only know how badly that definition makes me feel. Everybody is Somebody. Somebody ought to be of importance to at least one person in her or his world. Most of us are fortunate enough to have many others in our world who find us important to them. How is it that some people are considered a Nobody?

How many of us have seen on TV a homeless person stretched out over a heat grate on a cold night and feel sorry for that man or woman? Then what? Do we act on our feelings? I know I never go beyond feeling sorry, although I know I also feel kind of helpless. Maybe if I feel kind of helpless, that will be my excuse for doing nothing. How far can a single, caring person go in helping people others call a Nobody or a Loser or, as Webster says, a person of no importance?

Apparently, many single, caring people do just that – and they show it by joining with others who care for the "down and out." Many people who belong to large or small organizations go beyond just feeling bad for the homeless and other people in great need of the basics of life – food, shelter and clothing – they do something about it. They act on their feelings. One prime example of such a group is The Salvation Army. Another is God's Pit Crew. Add Soup Kitchens and Food Pantries to the caring givers and all the others at work throughout the country whose goal is to make sure no one is a Nobody. The caring people of central Pennsylvania are generous with their time for others. Good jobs are scarce and few have extra-money to spend on other people. Yet when tragedy strikes in a community, the first to respond to the needs of others are those who, themselves, have their own needs. And so, they give what they have, they comfort those in need and are generous with their time. The caring in this area is something special.

There is no way for sure to measure the good that may come out of activating one's feelings. We want to believe that givers' caring ways will rub off on those who turn away from people they consider Nobodies or persons of no importance.

There is no place I know of in the psychology of Alfred Adler or Rudolf Dreikurs that refers to a human being as Nobody or a person of no importance. Adler and Dreikurs had a holistic approach to human beings in a social world. By holistic, they mean that every human, as an individual being, cannot be divided into parts in order to be understood. A human being cannot be sectioned off - not by appearance alone, or one's grammar – not by their dress or wallet contents - or lack of money in their wallets, their past employment or non-employment, their love life or their family make-up. We cannot know a person unless we look at him or her as a whole functioning person with a heart that beats and a need to fit – to belong – in this world. We have to get better at including and less better at excluding.

All of those traits and possessions need to be combined - sort of like making sure all the ingredients needed for a favorite recipe are combined together, stirred, tasted for more salt or pepper, stirred some more and eventually announced as perfect. People who are down on their luck and are homeless cannot be understood by the one and only fact we know - that they are, at present, homeless. The individual, then, is something like a recipe. We can only really know others by knowing more than one ingredient of their human self.

Those who act on their feelings in order to give value to a human being in dire need of help are my heroes. They make everybody a Somebody.

Remember Russell – the young teenager who was called Blimp by his peers and many others in the community? I can describe Russell's life from the time on the sidewalk when I was 12 and he was being bullied by two older boys. I can also describe his life as an adult.

To many in our small town, Russell was a Nobody. Well, let's hope he was Somebody to his parents. Since I was just 12 and new to the school and community, my mother did not want me to "tell" the police about Russell's struggle with the bullies. She felt I could end up in the hands of those bullies some day. How did she come to that conclusion? She talked with the Police Chief. The Chief was a nice-enough man yet he expressed his reluctance to interfere so long as Blimp (his name for Russell) wasn't showing any injuries. The Chief was a proponent of Boys Will Be Boys. In all fairness to the Chief, he promised to keep his eye on the situation.

The next thing my mother did was to talk with one of my teachers. She didn't want to talk on the telephone with a teacher because our family had what was called a "party line." This means that while we're having a phone conversation with someone, others on our party line could pick up their phone and listen to our conversation. What? You ask. Yes, that's the way it was for those who could not afford a private line. Anyway, people on your party line were supposed to be respectful when they discovered their line was already being used. They were supposed to hang up immediately and wait a few minutes before trying again. Some did. Some didn't. The ones who didn't follow the rules were the ones who spread rumors. Now <u>that</u> was serious misbehavior in those days.

Back to Russell's situation with those two bullies. My mother chose not to phone my English teacher to discuss those bullies. Instead, she walked to my new school at the end of the school day to meet with her. My English teacher repeated what the Police Chief had said – that those two bullies are really bad and the teachers are all counting the days when they drop out of school. She also said some of the teachers are afraid of those bullies but that she was not.

Her husband held the top position as Superintendent of All County Schools. I guess she felt protected.

And so, Russell continued to carry the bullies on his back whenever they beckoned him. I kept my distance as my mother advised. On the rare occasion when I passed Russell by himself on the sidewalk, I always said, "Hi" and he always said "Hi" back – but he never made eye contact. When I saw him on the sidewalk carrying those two goons on his back, he never responded to my, "Hi," although the bullies always laughed at me and made unmentionable remarks as they passed by.

When I graduated, married and moved away, I lost contact with Russell. My mother kept me posted, however, and Russell seemed freer of the bullies who were seen with him less often around town. Eventually, Russell married a nice young woman and they continued to live in the second floor apartment his parents had lived in. One day when I visited my mother, she told me Russell and his wife were going to have a baby. And that he was so excited. Russell was now Somebody as well as Somebody's soon-to-be father.

The baby girl was adored by Russell and his wife. Unfortunately, she was born with a defective heart. She had several surgeries and lived less than a year. It was devastating to Russell and his wife. Somehow, people in the town woke up and rallied round them. At long last, they expressed caring. Then Russell's wife became seriously ill and the town cared again. The Chief of Police had a meeting with Russell. Next thing people knew, Russell had joined the town's police force and was directing traffic at the two local churches on Sunday mornings. He wore his uniform proudly. He was free of his bullies. He had been an infant's Daddy for almost a year. His wife loved him. The community cared. Against all odds, Russell demonstrated what a survivor is.

Even though Russell died before he reached 40, he had become a Somebody after all.

O comes next - UhOh

O

OBEY

When parents are asked this question, "Do you want your children to obey you or do you want to be a parent who influences your children by being an example of good behavior?," almost all say they want to influence their kids. Then when asked how and why they would want to influence them, a few squirmed in their chairs until one brave Dad named Hank asked, "Do you mean I want them to behave like me – you know – like not swear in front of them and not drink OJ right from the carton?"

By now, we're all smiling – getting loosened up for a dive into the uncomfortable part of being a parent or a teacher or any other role model whenever kids are watching an adult's behavior.

So here goes the dive into the uncomfortable.

"Hank, your idea makes sense. You want to make a good impression in front of your kids. That's good."

Hank smiles and puffs out his chest – a happy guy. He took a chance and made a good impression. He folds his arms in front of his chest and waits for a response.

"You wanted your kids to know that you know how to behave in, what we could call a social setting. The family is a social setting. The kitchen is a kind of social setting, isn't it?"

"Sure is," Hank said, "Lotsa people eating pizza all the time. Full House is another name for our kitchen."

Everyone enjoys Hank's humor. Then we move on.

Now my question for Hank quiets him for about 15 seconds. "You behaved well in the kitchen in front of your son, right? Do you behave the same way when your son is not in the kitchen with you?"

"Waddaya mean?"

"Let me ask in a different way. Did you ever swear in the kitchen and did you ever drink orange juice right from the carton?"

The whole group starts laughing as Hank stands up, turns to face them and says, "Guilty! Guilty as charged!" Everyone gives Hank a hand.

Then I ask for a volunteer to role play with me. Sheila hops up and we begin a skit. I tell her I'm her mother and she's my 14 year old daughter. We are having a little argument about nutrition and weight loss. My daughter prefers nachos, Fritos and Pepsi for breakfast while I insist she eat one egg and a banana and drinks cranberry juice. I pretend I'm setting the same healthy food in front of both of us. We play out the role – she's pouting and I'm a happy mother, enjoying nutritious food.

Now my pretend daughter waves "bye" to me and heads out the door with her backpack, on her way to catch the school bus.

I, as her mother, watch out the window as my daughter gets on the bus and is soon out of sight. I, as her mother, rush to the fridge for a Pepsi and a candy bar. I rummage through a cabinet for the chips. Now I'm all set for my breakfast.

It takes awhile to create order since everyone is laughing.

They all admit to being guilty of misbehaving in similar ways when their kids aren't watching.

We really want our kids to obey us so we model good behavior while they're watching. Do we really believe our kids intend to obey us when they're already suspicious of what we actually DO?

What kids will do, however, is at least listen when their parents admit they sometimes misbehave. Be honest with your kids. If you tell your kids you quit smoking (and didn't), won't your kids find out that you are still smoking? What about the smell? The pack of opened Camels on the car floor? Your breath when you give the kids a hello hug?

Admit to some of your bad habits. As a parent, however, you still maintain the right to ask better behavior of your kids. What's wrong with hoping your kids will go up a notch or two in good behavior and a few notches above you in social skills and caring about others? Life is too short for family members to constantly be chewing at one another. Pick your battles wisely and accept a small amount of non-fatal mischief and fibs along the way.

In my years of offering parenting courses and parent workshops, the above scene plays out every time – different people, different walks of life but the same kinds of situations between kids and parents.

The moral of this story is that parents really want their kids to obey them. The truth is that kids don't obey us. They do not obey us! They may pretend to obey while we are within arm's reach of them but the minute they're out of sight, they do, basically, what they already planned to do.

Let's return to school. There is a big difference between demanding obedience and going the influence route. Life is better in school classrooms when the teacher's influence begins with the following 4th grade to middle school example:

Day I of a new school year – The teacher describes the kind of year they're going to have together. Students will have rights and responsibilities, written personal goals, form friendships, a cooperation trumps competition theme, participate in a class meeting twice a month, understand and agree to logical consequences for breaking a class rule. Class rules will be written and posted by the class Day 2 of a new school year with the consequences for rules broken understood ahead of time. Students will sign the Rules and Consequences chart to indicate they participated in the development of behavior expectations. No surprises. For 180 days.

The teacher is firm and confident as well as smiling and caring.

Next letter is going to be linked with our A word, our R word and our W word. Turn now to the letter **P**

P

POWER

The P word is Power. Another word almost like Power is Control. We can use both those words in this exploration since they are so alike in meaning. Out of respect for the brilliant work of Rudolf Dreikurs and others, I am beginning this section with the word Power, although I prefer to use the term Control. For my use with today's kids and adults, Control seems more relevant.

Where on earth is the human being who doesn't want some control in the family, in school, in social situations, at work and in other aspects of life. You may have thought, "No, she's wrong. I'm not like that." Perhaps that response really means, "Yes, I want control but that doesn't work in my family." Or, "I get more attention by being shy. The focus is on me lots of times." These are just a few examples of a person who isn't buying the premise that all human beings want and need some control – some power – over other people and situations. Yet, if you are alive, you want some control over your life. If you are ill with a serious or terminal disease, you want some control - over your medication, your demand for room temperature, your nurses and your caretakers. Until we take our last breath, we want some control over our life situations.

The main thing about the need for control is that we all want it, and we all get it - one way or another. For example, when we feel we aren't gaining enough of it –or that we aren't getting any at all - that's when misbehavior arrives.

Let's get acquainted with one of the most brilliant concepts I ever came across and embraced-for-life in the field of human behavior. It was conceived by Alfred Adler and activated for use by Rudof Dreikurs. There was a major acceptance of these concepts and practical use of them first with parents struggling with misbehaving children, world-wide! Can you imagine that? A movement that began in Austria, spread throughout Europe after the first World War and landed in the good old USA just before WWII. After the second World War ended, another brilliant doctor named Heinz Ansbacher took Adler's work, which was mostly written in German, and translated it into English. Ansbacher made Adler's work easy to read, easy to learn and easy for Dreikurs to conduct countless seminars for American parents – highly successful seminars.

As you can tell by now, I do not want this book to be text-bookish, along with footnotes and a format that is like many other non-fiction books. I tend to write in a conversational style, without complex terminology and strict adherence to conventional rules. Still, without my introduction to Adler, Dreikurs and Ansbacher in the 1970's, including the historical and common sense aspect of their work, I never would have gained what I did – a good understanding of human behavior that helped me to help parents, teachers and students.

A person who influenced me most as an educator and "regular person," is Dr. Stanley Dubelle. Dr. Dubelle was Assistant Superintendent in my first school district. Let me give you one example of *his* behavior the first time I met him. If you are a classroom teacher and a new top administrator comes to town, you are a bit nervous about potential changes that may occur. Still, teachers tended not to worry about the new guy because administrators rarely visited the schools, much less visited classrooms. Administrators were office people. What a surprise awaited them when Dr. D arrived!

The day I met the new man in town was when I was a kindergarten teacher. The kindergartners and I were engaged, as always, in several activities all at once. The room was a beehive of meaningful activity with everyone behaving well and getting along, sharing and caring and learning (our motto). That's the moment a bang/bang/bang hit the closed door and in walked this unknown man, calling out, "Hi boys and girls. I'm Mr. Dubelle and I am your teacher's boss. Do you think I'm a bossy boss?"

The kids were all excited and laughing. They shouted back, "Yes!!!" With that, my boss borrowed a jump rope from one of the boys and began to jump rope. Since we only had four jump ropes, three others joined the new Assistant Superintendent and jumped rope round the room, having the time of their lives.

I was – to put it mildly – stunned. Hopeful, too, and impressed - wondering how the other teachers were going to handle the banging on the door and the noisy entrance of the new Assistant Superintendent. I had already figured out who would like him, who would fear him and those who were on the doubting fence. And at lunchtime in the faculty room, I found out I was right.

When Dr. Dubelle went on to be Superintendent of the larger Wilson School District, I followed him there a few years later. It was the best choice for me, even though he retired 10 years later and I continued on.

I'll never forget my introduction to the person who influenced me most as an educator. Dr. D trusted me to take Adler, Dreikurs and Ansbacher with me and run. We were going to be the school district where misbehavior was not common and higher levels of learning were achieved within one year. Most of all, we would create an environment where kids felt liked, respected and cared about and where the curriculum was developmentally appropriate, kindergarten through grade 6. Parents became partners and many parent groups were formed in support of our plans. Parenting classes became popular and important.

We never expected our district to be problem-free. With diversity in family life and socio-economic variations and the special needs of some learners, challenges will always exist. Still, we greatly reduced the behavioral problems and greatly increased academic achievement. Parents and teachers were supportive and active on behalf of their children and their students.

Teachers finally had a welcome control over some parts of the curriculum. For example, teachers were encouraged to develop a unit of study that was unique and important to them – one developed a unit she called, "The Beaches of the West Coast of Florida." Another teacher created a unit called, "Facts, Fun and Figures About Baseball, Football and Soccer." Teachers could teach their personal, highly individualized unit of study for a time frame of three to five school days once the unit was developed and then approved by the principal. A hands-on approach with touchable items and mementoes from the teacher's trips and experiences would also include relevant technology, literacy, math and science teachings for that grade level. There wasn't a bored moment for kids or teachers. Enthusiasm and good behavior hit a high note. Giving teachers and kids some power or control over their teaching and learning is what Adler was all about. Self-discipline can be a wonderful by-product of good behavior. Creating and developing balance in adults and their children was a key to developing control over one's behavior.

A new requirement for teachers was to develop class rules with their students – no more than four or five rules. Each broken rule was to have a logical consequence, and was to be understood by the students. Each student signed the large list of rules, indicating he or she read the rules and consequences and understood them. Consequences were to be as closely aligned to the rule as possible. A consequence is not punishment and even the kindergartners learned to grasp the difference. What is the difference? Punishment is meted out for an infraction, yet has no relevance to the infraction. A consequence has a direct relationship to the infraction. Example: Drop and break something you were not supposed to touch – clean up the pieces and try to glue them together or "work off" the cost to buy another one if you don't have the cash.

Back to classroom rules. Each rule was numbered, 1,2,3,4 or 5. To minimize talking, scolding and yackety-yacking to the students most likely to break a rule, the teacher just says, "Betsyann, that's number three." Teacher will apply the consequence to Betsyann if she misbehaves a second time that day. Betsyann knows exactly what the score is. There are never surprises when an Adlerian approach to education is introduced and followed consistently.

We will be adding the word **Power or Control** to one already explored – the word **Attention**. The other two words to be added are the letters R and W. A key and useful Adler/Dreikurs concept will come together following the letter Z.

Moving on to **Q**

QUANTITY

There has been a great deal of debate about Quantity vs Quality in the early years of a child's life – the main issue being this: Is Quality time enough for parents in caring for their child from birth to three or is Quantity time the most important? The real issue began after WWII when women who were mothers struggled about continuing to work outside the home while a relative or "sitter" took care of the children. It appears that as many as half of those working mothers continued in their jobs while half quit their jobs and returned to the home and their young child or children. Statistics differ, although let's stick with an almost half and half divide.

It may seem difficult for me to remain neutral since I chose to stay home with our three young children while my husband worked at three jobs. We chose both quality and quantity time with our kids and never looked back with regret. Like most women in those days and these days, I wanted it all yet believed deeply that I had to delay work outside the home. I felt confident enough that I could have it all eventually, just not all at once. I chose the path I wanted most – being a wife and mother - and then I told myself that a meaningful career would be waiting for me after the children were older and doing well in and out of school.

I am not judging the decisions of women who are mothers of young children. I am also not judging the decisions of women who chose a career during their childrens' early childhood years. Who am

I to judge when I had only one experience – to remain at home with the children while my husband took on three jobs?

A new book has been published, titled *Being There*. The author is Erika Komisar. You may have seen her on TV, describing her book. She writes things like, "Put down the phone. Pick up the kids." She also believes our society devalues mothering. If you are struggling with this issue, of home vs career outside the home, Komisar's book could be helpful.

On a personal level, my daughter became a single mother for seven years. She raised our granddaughter during those years until she met and married the love of her life. We couldn't ask for a more wonderful daughter, granddaughter and son-in-law.

If the reader feels I lean towards one parent remaining at home during those first three-to-five years of their children's life, you're on to something. I do. Still, I know and have become friends with women who were called "working mothers" with growing and now adult children who seem to have turned out well. I consider myself fortunate that my husband was able to take on three jobs and still continue to be a wonderful Dad.

I hesitate to describe my personal journey yet I'd like to demonstrate that a wife and mother of young children can "have it all" – just not all at the same time. I was fortunate to be able to "have it all" - over a long period of time. From the age of nine I wanted to go to college to become a school teacher. Before I was nine, I fully intended to become the first female baseball pitcher in Major League history. Once reality set in, I set my sights on becoming a teacher and a mother.

I do believe it has to be difficult on a marriage, preschoolers and school-age children when working outside the home, as well as, managing the daily needs of everyone. Daily needs include chores such as cooking, cleaning, grocery shopping, laundry, money issues, holiday dinners, birthday parties, volunteering at school, making Halloween costumes, buying Valentine cards for children's school parties, making a treat to take to school on your kids' birthdays, nursing sick children and spouse to good health, going to work while you're sick, making doctor and dentist appointments, chauffeuring the kids to soccer practice – and on and on. No exaggeration with that long sentence.

In my later work outside the home, I came upon just two fathers who happily called themselves Daddy Mom. They were the main parent during daytime hours while both parents did an admirable job with the kids in the evening and on weekends. One of these couples took the parenting course and were quite fascinating to the other parents in the group.

The Quantity/Quality time issue will likely remain with us until longitudinal studies are published and do not reveal bias in any way. By long-term, I mean studies that span participants' early childhood through at least 25 to 30 years of age. Perhaps there are already studies underway. I sure hope so. Otherwise, I won't be around to read the results. I want to be around!

Of all the alphabet letters, the letter Q for Quality has the shortest exploration. I like to think I said what I needed to say and moved on.

Turn to the letter **R**

R

REVENGE

Revenge is the harshest, most hurtful word in our A to Z alphabet. It is serious misbehavior. Revengeful behavior is never good behavior. It is intended to hurt and hurt badly and is used by the avenging person as a way of getting even. Typically, revengeful behavior is misguided, in that the person at the receiving end of that misbehavior is totally innocent of what he's accused of doing. Either way, innocent or guilty of wronging another, it can be fatal. Revenge will have its outlet. It's almost impossible to intervene or stop it from being carried out once the seed of revenge is planted in someone's brain.

We now have the third of the four words needed to complete something Adler and later, Dreikurs, called, The Four Goals of Misbehavior. If you are able to grasp those four goals and carry them with you for the rest of your life, you will be able to minimize your verbal and behavioral bad times with others and maximize your success with relationships and situations that challenge you.

Let the Good Times Roll may be a bit too premature with hope. Mastering the Four Goals of Misbehavior requires three things: an understanding of each one and how they are hierarchically descending in that they move from Goal 1 to 2 to 3 and land at 4. The second thing required in mastering the Goals is an acceptance – can you see the logic in them? The purpose? Are they worthwhile for you in dealing with children and adults of all ages who misbehave with you? The third thing required is their use. Do you believe you can learn how to use them in a situation where misbehavior is a problem to you? Remember, Individual Psychology is also known as the Psychology of Use. It's supposed to be rather easy to use since it is based on human behavior, misbehavior and common sense. Still, mastering it requires those three main things.

How many verbal phrases and physical force are used EVERY DAY on misbehavior by teachers, mothers, fathers, step-parents, grandparents, day care staff, husbands, wives, significant others, caretakers/caregivers/bus drivers – and others you are welcome to add to the list.

Here are a few phrases used when confronted with someone who is misbehaving.

Why are you doing that?

Are you trying to make me mad?

Are you trying to make me look like a bad person?

How dare you look at me like that!

How many times must I tell you to come to dinner?

How many times must I tell you to _____ (add 20 more here)

And who died and made you a saint?

With your big butt sticking out, why'd you think you'd look good in *that*?

Who made you Judy Garland? The Wicked Witch of the North?

Who'd want to go out with *you*, much less kiss you?

Whoever ate that last piece of cake is getting a whupping! Who did it?

I am sick and tired of looking at your unmade bed. What if Grandma visits?

Wherever did you get such a horrible big mouth?

I'm damn sick and tired of hearing you swear like that.

Now look what you did! You always drop something on the floor. Clutz!

If I continue typing examples, I'll need another ream of paper and I'll also either bore you to death or have you rolling on the floor when you "hear" yourself talking - so let's begin now by listing the first three Goals of Misbehavior. Once you learn how to use the Goals, EVERY SINGLE kind of misbehavior fits one of the Goals. Instead of resorting to all those weak, whiney and ineffective phrases such as those above, all you'll ever need is four goals and a silent question: Which one is he after? Then your responses to the misbehavin' person will be more appropriate and more effective.

ATTENTION
CONTROL or POWER
REVENGE
W

And there you *almost* have it, folks. For now we need to concentrate on the Goal of Misbehavior called Revenge.

A boy of about 11 was riding his bike all around the campground, annoying and then angering most of the people at their campsites. He would act like he was going to run the people over – and then laugh and pull the other way just before running into them. My husband calls kids like that brats. I call them misbehavin' and then I try to figure out what they're after.

Anyway, my husband couldn't help himself after watching that boy's bike- riding "tricks" so he asked the boy where his mother was and the boy told him it was none of his business. He used his tall finger to make his point as he sped off on his bike.

I turned away. It wasn't funny but I had to laugh into my sleeve. My husband didn't find my behavior funny so I used my best active listening skill to say, "You're right. It isn't funny." My husband semi-smiled and we walked on. That afternoon, I was lying on our RV bed reading and I heard a funny sound – I couldn't place it and assumed it was our camping neighbor playing some kind of music turned down low. At least that's what it sounded like to me. Still, I was curious and looked out the window of the RV and saw THAT BRAT kid! He had just finished letting all the air out of two of our tires!

That wasn't funny.

I ran out but he was far away by then.

My husband came back shortly after the brat took off and I told him what had happened. He was – well, in a word, he was furious. After he calmed down, we both agreed the situation was better than if the boy had slashed the tires. Still, I felt we should find out which campsite he's at and talk with his mother or father. Somehow, I figured the kid was either after the goal of Power or Revenge. This wasn't a good time for me to reveal that to my husband.

When I suggested we find the parents and talk with them, my husband said, "Oh, I already talked with his mother. About his bike behavior. I found her in site 38. There's no father in the picture, so I talked with her. She wasn't really useful – kind of overwhelmed with the kid's constant misbehavior. She seemed nice enough but nothing was solved. Now that I know we need air in the tires, I guess I'll do that myself."

And my husband did just that. With the RV tires filled with new air, we left the next morning for our end destination in Florida to continue our retirement journey. On the way to the campground exit, we saw the boy on his bike. He stopped as we passed him on my side of the RV. I smiled and waved to him. He did not wave back. After all, his goal was revenge. He wanted me to cry or yell or threaten him. I wanted him to know his misbehavior didn't work on us and that we fixed the problem and silently wished him a better day. Had we been able to talk with him privately, I'd have done a better job than just smiling and waving a friendly goodbye.

Attention-seeking was not likely positive for him after years of trying and failing so the boy turned to negative attention-getting. It looks like that wasn't working too well, either, so the boy went deeper and into the Power or Control Goal. It probably worked with his mother so he tried it on others who questioned his Power or Control over others. When his control over others (my husband talking to his mother about his misbehavior) was weakened, the boy slipped into the Revenge Goal. He tried to hurt us by flattening our tires. He did a good job of it but as we left the campground, he could tell we had not been too inconvenienced by the flat tires – another indication that the boy lacked – in our case - the ability to win through revenge. All of this will make more sense as we move on.

For the boy's sake, I did the unexpected. I smiled. I gave him a friendly wave. Doing the Unexpected works most of the time, and most of the time is better than none of the time.

How did I decide that boy's Goal of Misbehavior was Revenge? First of all, his bike- riding tricks were annoying yet they weren't getting him any positive attention so he slipped down into the Power or Control Goal. When he didn't achieve any sense of control over my husband when he saw my husband talking with his mother, he had to punish my husband. And the boy let all the air out of our RV tires.

I believe the boy didn't want me to see him actually "in the act." He wanted no "witness." I believe he just wanted us to figure out he was the one who did it to punish us. Smart kid that he was, he wanted to outsmart us – the ones with the real power. He knew we'd know he did the deed – but we could never prove it. He was mistaken. I heard it and I saw it. And so, his pattern of misbehavior suggests there'll be a whole lot of "Revenging" going on.

In order for me to get a better understanding of the goal of Revenge in different cultures than the ones I know best (I claim to be no expert), I turned to the books written by David Ignatius. I just finished *Blood Money* and recommend it highly. Ignatius seems to be the most readable and knowledgeable person I've come upon in regard to major revengeful behavior throughout much of the Middle East. While the book you're reading now is not written to be a geo-political examination of world-wide proportions, I feel compelled to mention how acts of revenge throughout the world fit right in with the Four Goals of Misbehavior.

On to the first letter of my second favorite place - **S**

S

SCHOOL

My second-favorite place on earth is school. My #1 favorite is home. Home is wherever my husband and I happen to be. Home is also wherever our children, their spouses, our granddaughter and her husband and our great-grandson, Jackson, happen to be, at any given time.

My husband and I have moved 13 or 14 times during our 59 years of marriage. As you can tell, I've almost lost an accurate account. With all our moving around when our children were in school, we remained in the same county in Pennsylvania so our children would have a stable Kindergarten to 12th grade education. It worked well for our kids – they were fortunate to be able to attend and graduate from top public schools.

My personal comments are a segue to my second-favorite place – School!

Public schools are examples of extremes in the quality of education across our country that we are witnessing and experiencing today. That is not to say private and parochial schools *are all* of the same educational quality either, or that home-schooling is of *the same* quality in every home situation. I do believe today's public schools are generally functioning at a lower level than they did in the distant past. Twice in my career, I was asked to evaluate schools that sought to be awarded a Blue Ribbon status school. I've made many visits to schools from Texas to Louisiana, to Maryland, other Pennsylvania Schools and up to Long Island, NY. Not boasting here – just indicating I'm not a novice in evaluating the quality of schools. I'm also old enough to have no fear of offending the offenders! I may have a high-number birthday coming up although in my mind and with the joy of living I experience every day, I am 41. Again.

In my visits and evaluations of school quality and achievement I have not come upon "bad" schools, although the closest to being inferior to others were schools located in cities with a high population of needy kids. That's to be expected, not because the students are lacking in intelligence and a hunger to learn. Rather, a number of those schools seem to be run by administrators and Boards of Education who lack the qualities necessary for leadership. Far too many school districts seem to be led by individuals lacking in knowledge and caring. In fairness to those leaders who really do give their best for kids in school, there's another reason why public schools are in trouble. Often, the poor quality of education in far too many schools is due to a lack of essential funding determined by people we elect – individuals who seem to have no clue as to how children learn and what they need in a good, safe, environment with caring teachers and essential equipment and supplies. They should want the best and safest social environment possible within the walls of a building called a public school.

The problems facing public education are enormous. I fear the decline in public schooling will continue if we continue to hire school leaders with almost no knowledge of the learner, K-12, and almost no knowledge of a curriculum that is developmentally appropriate, stimulating, important and worth learning. It seems we no longer teach for mastery of skills but rather loosely introduce this and that and then move on. That's no way to prepare our future adults for employment, the military or an education that requires basic knowledge and skills. Problems will continue if we choose to elect and hire people to important roles who are unqualified for the job.

Apologies, in advance, to those high-functioning and caring

school leaders and elected officials who perform at high levels! There are some. They deserve our recognition and appreciation. Still, it is my opinion that they are – sad to say - in the minority. The best, brightest and most caring educational leaders are the few bright lights among the many low lumens. That's not acceptable.

In addition to educational leadership – or lack thereof - today's public schools are less safe from the outside world as well as less safe within the halls and walls of the classrooms. Student misbehavior is more serious than it was decades ago. Teachers and other staff are also finding their working environment less safe. Student achievement and success have decreased. School taxes continue to increase to unaffordable costs for the majority of taxpayers in cities and towns across the nation. We are now paying more to operate inferior schools than we paid when we were operating superior schools. Yes, I allowed for adjustments over time.

This place called school should be a place where, when a kid crosses the threshold of the main entrance and walks through the hall to a classroom, he or she is greeted by name from at least one adult. Another student saying, "Hi Charlie" would be nice, too. All kids should be dressed appropriately for school learning and not distracted by social and personal reasons as an excuse for not learning. That kid should have wakened in the morning in his homey home by at least one adult who loves and cares about him, helped him get a nutritious breakfast and helped pack a balanced lunch (or given him lunch $$). He should have received a hug or a kiss "goodbye" unless he thinks he is too old for that mush. A smile alone could do for teenagers. A fist bump, perhaps? Sometimes teenagers even smile *and* fist-bump back. Savor that morning if it comes your way.

And forgive me for saying it one more time – when entering a school building for a regular school day, please do not allow kids to dress like they're going to the beach.

Public Schools have been around for more than 120 years . They began by establishing high schools in the late 1800s. Believe it or not, the first Charter School saw its beginning in the state of Minnesota in the early 1950s. Vocational Schools were pretty well-established between WWI and the Great Depression. More recently, Magnet Schools, Cyber Schools, and others were established. Home-schooling continues to grow in numbers. Catholic and other religious-based schools have been in existence for a long time. If you need more history on the advent of public, private and parochial schools, check with Dr. Google.

I believe the teaching-learning process has existed forever. The first teachers were most likely parents who lived in caves, carried a club and showed their kids how to write and draw on the walls.

This place called school is not always in a school building, although we tend to think of schools that way. Let's continue to invent better ways to educate today's children – with the best of the best adults leading the way as partners to their children's teachers – and with affordable school/property taxes. Remember, also, to get out and vote! Find out which state, local and national candidates seem best for public education. Ask them what they know about child development of children ages 4 to 18. Ask them what they know about curriculum, K-12, and if they know what developmentally appropriately curriculum means. Ask them about their own school experiences.

Get out and vote. Just remember to vote smart - and hire smart, as well. If our schools could speak right now, they'd say, "thank you."

It's almost **T** time

T

TALKING

TALK, TALK, TALK, YACKETY YACK, TALK, TALK

How often do you wish you were an escape artist when a gabby person is approaching you and you know what that means. It means at least an extra 15 minutes of your valuable time wasted.

Today my best friend, Mary, is the victim of a Yackety Yacker.

"Oh, hi there Mary! How wonderful to see you again! What are you doing in this part of town? Don't you live in one of those little duplexes over near Fritzville? However can you get all your furniture in one of their tiny living rooms? They're rent-controlled, aren't they – oh, sorry – none of my business how are your children? J.C. and Manny? My Henry the Third has been accepted to West Point – well, not quite – but almost and by the way, my Tiffany has started dating they date early these days, don't they and Henry the Second wasn't too happy that I gave Tiff the okay because he was in the Bahamas when Tiff asked about dating but someone has to make a decision when the other is off on business don't you think?"

Mrs. Henry Hightower the Second just ran out of breath. That gives Mary a chance to tell her she has an important engagement in five minutes.

As Mary turns to walk away, Mrs. Henry Hightower the Second shouts to her, "Where *is* your important engagement? *Who* is it with?"

Mary, known for always keeping 'em guessing, just gives her that Mona Lisa smile, wiggles her eyebrows and waves goodbye.

Every once-in-awhile we have to give ourselves that inner smile that helps us to survive a conversation with someone who talks too much, too fast and holds us hostage for too long.

In a nutshell, too many adults talk too much - in a group social setting, adults we bump into on the sidewalk (as did Mary), politicians, some pastors, most talk-show hosts/hostesses, TV news analysts, coaches – and on and on – are often guilty of talking too much – which in my book, is misbehavior. Why? When the talker goes on and on and the listener's eyes start to glaze over while her body language shouts – no! It begs! - for a fast getaway, the talker is misbehaving. That's when the talker must let the person go. Oh but no. The talker doesn't do that. The talker does what he or she was born to do. Talk, Talk, Talk.

That's misbehavior. That's attention-seeking. That's control. The extreme talker can't get enough attention. Or, maybe it's a control-thing. Either Goal 1 or Goal 2 misbehavior. It's often both. The extreme talker goes back and forth on a needs basis and holds you hostage until she's ready to let you go.

Parents and teachers are especially good at talking too much. How many minutes in a child's school day – or a Saturday at home – does the child actually talk – you know – like say something other than, "I didn't do it!" or ""Lemme alone," or "Huh?" How much meaningful time does each child have in any given school day to actually speak or express herself verbally or indicate she knows the answer, if only you'd listen?

Teachers – we love you dearly - yet please give your students more chances to speak in the classroom. It is absolutely essential for classroom teachers to make sure every student is encouraged and expected to make relevant verbal comments throughout the school week. It is especially essential for teachers to hear the thoughts and words from speech-impaired students, troubled students and quiet or shy students. When students are allowed to choose where they sit in the classroom, make sure those who tend to choose the back of the room are noticed and addressed by the teacher. Sometimes, when seating is a choice, the students with the most social or serious family problems sit in the back of the classroom. Not always, of course, but often enough for teachers to see a pattern.

I am fully aware that "Teaching to the Test" has become epidemic throughout the nation and that there is precious little time to do what really matters for a public school education. The developmentally inappropriate components of the standardized tests - required by states at certain grade levels – are bordering – in my opinion - on child abuse, especially at the elementary grade levels. There is no way that kind of testing can continue for much longer. By the time you read these words, the standardized testing currently required may be history. That would be a day to celebrate.

Moving on from the above commercial that helped me to vent my anger, let's return to the premise that teachers tend to do too much of the talking in classrooms. We can't let required inappropriate standardized testing to keep us from finding more ways for our students to have more "talk time" in class. Of course, talking and listening activities in a social setting away from computers and other electronics mean more planning for the teacher. Yet in the end, how are today's school kids going to learn how to develop human relationships, problem-solving with others and speaking and listening skills if most of their school hours are involved with a computer screen and other visuals – mostly electronic?

During teacher inservice days, grade level teams can bring ideas to share and develop to use throughout the school year. These ideas would require more face time with each other and less face time with a machine. Sure, computers are amazing – however, the entire class made up of human beings talking, listening and learning together are even more amazing.

Here's a simple idea for teachers to use at any grade level, kindergarten through 12th grade. Modify as needed.

With kindergartners, we called it "Minuters," although in the beginning of the school year, we called it "Half-Minuters." You've probably figured out that most kindergartners in the first half of the school year are not developmentally ready to express and sustain their thoughts for one minute in front of the class.

In a plastic jar, we placed about 25 strips of paper, each with a topic printed on it. All topics were appropriate. For example, one strip would say, *All about my favorite foods* or *My favorite vacation* or *Colors I like and colors I don't like* or *Things that scare me.*

The first half of the year, kindergartners had a half-minute to keep talking, plus a few responses to other kindergartners or questions from the teacher. If a child is struggling to sustain a full 30 seconds, the teacher can jump in and ask a relevant question – or call on someone else to question the talker at the front of the room.

Here are the steps that work well for Minuters with non-readers.

1. Teacher controls the jar with the topics.
2. A child either volunteers to be first or the teacher chooses someone.
3. Child goes to the front of the room, reaches into the jar and pulls out a topic. Teacher reads it for her (most Kindergartners are not readers, especially in the beginning of the year).
4. Teacher asks if the child can talk about "This is how I get ready for school." Rarely, will a child refuse, although some may require a little help. The teacher will then ask questions of the child to get him going – What's the first thing you do when you get out of bed? Be respectful and kind. Some kids have trouble being "on stage" to be judged by others – even five year olds. In time, they all come around.
5. Provide a timer that has a ring-ringer sound. Set it for 30 seconds. By mid-year, begin setting the timer for 60 seconds.

6. The speaker stops the moment the dinger goes off. That's the rule. Talk ends at 30 (or 60) seconds. Kindergartners learn what rules mean and what seconds mean.

7. In the beginning, teacher might only want to play Minuters one time in a day. Eventually increase the number of times to two or three per day.

8. To keep interest high, take an occasional break from this activity. The kids will let you know when they want to play it again.

9. Remember to refresh your supply of topics for the jar.

10. Make sure every child eventually gets several chances throughout the school year. Keep some kind of short record for each child. Don't write volumes about each child – just shorthand kinds of comments. Date them. They will be useful during parent conferences. Some amazing insights come out of this activity. Kids gain confidence and a sense of importance when they become comfortable with getting up front to talk. By the end of the school year, each child most likely has been up in front of the others a number of times, talking about a topic, answering questions and gaining a sense of telling time!

Children talking. A breath of fresh air! Children listening. They are following rules. They are becoming brave in front of others. They are not misbehaving. They are learning! No one can hide here! They all belong! They are, each of them, one essential piece of a jigsaw puzzle. They all fit!

The teacher is loving it.

When taking Minuters to 6th grade, we called it Topic and Time or "Ninety Seconders." In 8th grade, we introduced Minuters as "Don't Beat the Clock" or "Two Minuters" – topics that were selected a few days in advance. A presentation date was set. Students could also come up with their own topic, although that topic had to be approved in advance of the student's presentation. You can guess why – maybe they'd like to talk about why old guys take Viagra or ways to drive parents crazy. Kids will be kids when given too much free reign.

If this idea sounds like Show and Tell of years and years gone by, it has similarities. It's different, however, and it is important in the secondary grades as well as the elementary grades. Once technology arrived, Big Time, important parts of learning from and about others as well as gaining an opportunity to become a better listener and speaker were eliminated in most schools. No time for learning in a group without gadgets because much of our school day has to be in front of a computer.

Think of all the ways to encourage students at all grade levels to learn to function and eventually enjoy being at the front of the class, talking and becoming comfortable there - thinking on their feet, using proper grammar, learning how to use their voice more effectively – performing in front of a live audience and sharing information.

No grades are given for this kind of activity. At the elementary level, encourage applause after each student's presentation. Applause and high-fives may get too rowdy for secondary students. Come up with an appropriate show of appreciation or congratulations for the presenter.

Human beings are social creatures. As such they need human contact, conversations and activities with others. They are "socially connected" first in a family setting. They are socially connected in their school, their neighborhood, their place of worship, their community, their workplace and wherever else they have contact with others. Human beings have a deep, silent, sometimes hidden need to belong in any group to which they are assigned or choose to join. There is no greater need for human beings than to belong – to fit in – to connect with - to share ideas with – to argue with - to compare yourself with – to care about and to respect yourself and others.

An ideal social setting that encourages and enforces good behavior works! Please don't minimize the importance of students performing "live" in front of their classmates. Close down the computers for awhile.

Teachers are setting the stage. With a hand pointing to the rules chart, teacher reminds students of the rules without having to say a word. Teachers apply the consequences swiftly with either no words or soft-spoken words. Teacher moves on. No yelling at the students. No students yelling at other students. Teacher doing the unexpected and learning ways to defuse a potentially bad situation before it happens. Teacher using silence to get kids' attention.

Kids taking turns talking in a group setting. Everybody else listening. Kids asking questions of the presenter. The teacher talking less.

The class listening.

The teacher listening.

The teacher talking less!

I was forced to learn about U-Tube

Here's **U**

U

U-TUBE

Here we go – into the deep, deep forest of electronics and technology, hardware and software - with readers who know the pathways infinitely more than I do. Just when I learn something new-to-me with my computer, I feel like an advanced IT person like my grandson, Kyle. Unfortunately, what I just learned is now obsolete and I must learn a new way. I rely on my savvy daughter to help me when I'm really lost in the forest of technology. Bear with me, please, as I attempt to follow the readers on the pathways they know so well.

U-Tube is a concept that fascinated me from its beginning. Apparently it fascinated millions and millions of others, world-wide – and continues to fascinate on a daily basis. In 2005, three brilliant young men got together to create the You Tube Website, now popularly known as U-Tube.

This website is now viewed – get ready for this – more than **one billion** hours every day. Every day! That's 1,000, 000, 000+. Here's another amazing number – U-Tube is #2 as the most popular website, not just in the USA but in the world! Perhaps by the time this book is published, it'll be #1.

U-Tube videos make viewers laugh and cry. They also produce other emotions and behavior in-between. "Reality" videos become invasive when parents and their children keep "upping the ante" to show their viewers a bit too much of their lives. What they seem unable to do is offer a healthy amount of daily human interaction in the development of positive relationships. There could be a danger in the over-viewing of computer screen action. Whether or not readers agree with that statement, at least consider the almost hypnotic bond between a human being and a TV or computer screen. Sure, that's a relationship yet is that the kind of relationship we want our children to develop? How will a child's sustained relationship with a TV or computer affect his or her relationship with other human beings as she matures?

These are questions we didn't have to ask or answer as technology and electronic gadgets were being invented and developed. Their development was almost too fast and captivating for scientists and medical doctors and general society to study and evaluate. Are negative and unintended consequences measurable? Who could tell at the onset of these amazing technological advances that there could be a down-side to the overuse of children's relationships with metal, glass, batteries and other non-human components? If we are being fair, we can agree that the unintended consequences are not all positive. What is happening with children who sit mesmerized in front of a computer screen or a TV screen for hours, eyes almost unblinking, mouth part-way open and the rest of the body almost motionless? Kids are oblivious to another in the room or almost deaf to the voice of a parent or sibling making a comment or asking a question. People often refer to kids watching TV or their computer screen as being "glued to the screen." That's a fitting expression. To break that incredible physical, technological and emotional hold the computer and TV screen have on our kids almost takes a nearby fire alarm to break the spell.

We all know for sure that many parents use videos on the computer and programs on the TV as babysitters. Parents who acknowledge that their children watch way too much TV and too many computer websites can reduce the time their kids spend in front of a lighted screen. Who runs the family these days? Who is the adult in charge? Who in the family is setting fair and firm rules of behavior before their children enter formal schooling? Who is requiring brothers and sisters to develop good relationships from which good behavior can thrive? No child will go through childhood without occasional misbehavior. A little harmless mischief here and there can add spice to family life and be overlooked. True misbehavior, however, requires consequences and adult guidance to the one misbehaving.

The U-Tube creators certainly weren't misbehaving in 2005. They were inventing something spectacular - and are to be admired. Steve Chen, Chad Hurley and Jawed Karim gave our world technology to amaze and entertain us. Chad Hurley was born in the Pennsylvania city where I was born. Apparently, we don't share a similar brain.

I am in awe of the way three young men developed something amazing. They have taken children and adults into the deepest forest of technology where children, especially, love to live. Why would the kids want to return to a world of human beings interacting with each other without a handful of electronics at their fingertips? Still, the grandmother in me wishes for more daily balance in children's lives.

My wish is that children will also learn to find their way back from the forest in order to develop good relationships between and among other human beings. Where is the balance between technology and face-to-face human relationships? I'd say a greater part of a child's daily waking hours is filled with some kind of machine or electronic device. Kids seem to be missing out in the kind of important social interaction that used to be available to them - even required - at home and in school and in the community. Social interaction requires at least two people who are looking away from a lighted screen or monitor and developing human relationships. Technology, of course, includes I-Phones and texting, to which children and teens also appear to be addicted. Those concerns alone deserve their own attention.

There is a fascination with watching videos on U-tube made by parents who choose to live their family life in front of cameras. Is this the New Normal? vlogging is a new word for me. It isn't yet in the dictionary, although Dr. Google explained it for me. vlogging is a video concept that draws millions of viewers a day to watch the way participating individuals, including parents and children, are living their daily lives.

I know, I know. I am an old fogie who can't or won't accept this New Normal. I worry about the husband and wife relationship in those videos. I worry even more about the children who are growing up before a video camera. Children who experience early fame, fortune and adoration tend to struggle with life as an adult.

I watched two episodes of vlogging, and don't need the experience a third time. I am very happy without watching vlogging. I am never bored. I love and care about my husband and the way we are living our lives. We love and care about our children and grandchildren and our friends, as well. We could do without TV if it were not the fact that in the summertime, I have to watch the Pirates' games on Channel 659. In the fall and winter I have to watch college basketball on TV, especially the Tar Heels of UNC and the "Dukies." However, I watch no professional football. Too much dancing around, chest-thumping and spewing the F-word all around the stadium and too much off-the-field serious misbehavior – some of it felonious.

Yes, I know. I am an old fogie, who happens to be forty-one on the inside. Forever 41. Here's proof. Once or twice a year, my husband and I travel to Floyd, VA so I can do clogging to Bluegrass music.

Clogging, not vlogging. Give it a try.

On to **V** – only four more to go!

V

VARIANCE

Henry Hightower the Third sits in the principal's office for the second time this week. He claims he's innocent. The office secretary overhears him talking to himself. "I never touched that girl. I don't have to lower myself for a girl with a face like one of my father's Beagle hunting dogs." The secretary shakes her head as she continues working at her computer. She's heard Henry's declaration of innocence before. A few minutes later, the office door opens and Henry's parents rush in. Mrs. Hightower hurries over to Henry and hugs and comforts him, murmuring, "My poor baby. What is that girl lying about now?"

Mr. Hightower the Second approaches the secretary and asks when the principal is coming out of her office to discuss this false accusation. He says, "She's already five minutes late and I have a plane to catch in forty-five minutes. Can't you buzz her?" The secretary tells Mr. Hightower that Ms. Rodriguez is on a conference call and will be finished soon. She suggests he take a seat and wait in comfort. Mr. Hightower the Second's under-his-breath comment is that these waiting room chairs are unfit for his $1,200 suit.

Two minutes later, the inner door opens and a lovely Ms. Rodriguez welcomes the Hightowers to her inner office. Parents and son are invited to sit with her around a table. Ms. Rodriguez does not use her desk for parent conferences. She is not an intimidating administrator, although this is not the first time young Henry has been in trouble. She describes the reason Henry was sent to the office a second time that week. Both times were for touching the same girl inappropriately. Henry knows the school rules as well as the consequences. First time he broke the rule, the consequence was to write the offended person a letter of apology and the promise that he would never repeat that misbehavior. Never. A copy of that letter of apology was mailed to his parents, although they never saw it because young Henry had brought in the mail the day the letter was delivered. He destroyed it before his parents knew about it.

Henry's father insists he never received a letter. He didn't, of course, although the principal doesn't know this. Ms. Rodriguez produces a copy for him to read. He glances at it and then throws it across the table. His anger is increasing. "I can sue you for lying. We never got a letter." Ms. Rodriguez continues with Henry's second offense that week, which was the same as the first when his consequence was writing a letter of apology. She explains that the consequence for a second offense is a face-to-face apology, a two-day suspension and a 500 word essay on the ways he'll improve his social behavior in school.

That did it! Mr. Hightower the Second stood up, leaned over the table and shook his finger near the nose of Ms. Rodriguez. He shouted loud enough for the secretary to hear in the adjoining room. "Do you know who I am? Well, do you know who I am, Ms., Ms. – principal?" Before Ms. Rodriguez could respond, Mr. Hightower informed her he now had just forty-two minutes to catch a plane and that she had better drop all that damned punishment stuff right now. His son doesn't have to stoop that low. He has all the girls he wants on the other side of town.

Ms. Rodriguez keeps her cool. She attempts to explain that students are not being punished when they break a rule. Instead students agree to accept the consequences they approved at the beginning of the school year. "We make the rules together and then we develop the consequences. Consequences are directly tied to the rule that was broken. There are no surprises. The kids know what will happen. They all sign the rules chart. There is no punishment, only consequences."

Mr. Hightower chooses not to listen respectfully to the principal's explanation. He turns his back to her and speed dials his lawyer. As he begins his conversation with the lawyer, he is heard to say, "My kid would never rub a Latino girl. He can have any blue-eyed blond he wants. I want you to sue the principal whatshername...Ms. Hernandez or Ms. Alvarez...whatever. And then I want her fired. I never should have listened to my stupid wife. She's the one who insisted we send our kid to public school."

In a different school district in a different county, Mr. Kline begins his trip to the principal's office in a bad mood. His 8 year old daughter, Suzanne, told him she was going to have to sand her desk or pay for a new one. "What the hell kind of school does Suzanne go to?" he asks his girlfriend. "Whoever heard of making a girl do the job a school janitor should be doing?"

The first thing Mr. Kline said to the principal, Mr. Harvey, was the same question he had asked his girlfriend. "Whoever heard of making a girl do the job a school janitor should be doing?"

Mr. Harvey smiled and began to explain about rules and consequences. "Since Suzanne scratched her initials and a classmate's initials on the top of her desk, the consequence is to either sand out the initials or help to pay for someone else to sand it." Mr. Kline responded quickly, "You mean she doesn't have to buy a new desk?"

Mr. Harvey smiled again and assured Suzanne's father that the desk wasn't damaged to that extent. However, Suzanne helped to develop the class rules and consequences at the beginning of the school year. The consequence for Suzanne's carving misbehavior was to undo what she had carved.

"But she's a girl!" Mr. Kline shouted. "Besides, what's so bad about carving her initials and a boy's initials on her desk? Big whoop. That's just normal for girls her age – to start liking boys. No big deal. By the way, what's the guy's initials? Just wondering."

Mr. Harvey cleared his throat before saying, "Mr. Kline, the only classmate of Suzanne's with the initials she carved in a heart with hers belongs to… to…a girl."

Mr. Kline's breathing increased until he was soon huffing and puffing. "What kind of pervert school am I sending my kid to? If you ever tell anyone else about this, I'll go to the School Board and get you fired. And about the desk. I'll be here tomorrow after school to do the sanding myself."

"And bring your daughter with you. She is responsible for carving on her desk. She is responsible for fixing it. And remember, Mr. Kline, Suzanne is only eight years old. Please don't read anything into girls liking girls or boys liking boys. It's normal – please don't make something out of it. Suzanne is a lovely, caring little girl. She makes friends with girls and boys. Still, remember to bring her with you tomorrow. She is responsible for the carving."

"Like hell she's coming with me. She'll be grounded after school for the rest of the year. And you better keep quiet about this."

As Mr. Kline left in a hurry, Mr. Harvey sought comfort in a cup of hot coffee and a left-over donut from breakfast. He loosened a filling with his first bite – and then he wondered what was going to happen to him next. Being a Principal isn't easy, even for a minute.

Variances. Mr. Webster defines a Variance as *a degree of change or difference; permission to bypass regulations.*

More and more parents are definitely attempting to bail out their kids when a school rule is broken and an automatic consequence is applied. The most common approach is for irate parents to threaten a lawsuit and/or to get the principal or classroom teacher fired. Parents want to bend the school rules and eliminate what they call punishment. They won't hear the value of students and teachers and principals developing rules, agreeing to the rules and the logical consequences for breaking a rule.

The Hightowers saw no short or long-term value to their son's signature on the high school rules chart. Mr. Kline saw no value to his daughter's signature on her classroom rules chart. What those parents saw is something indelible – something they don't want on permanent school records. Those parents – and thousands more like them – rarely allow the principals to explain that those kinds of situations would not appear on school records and would not follow them to any kind of post-high school experience. However, if laws are broken and law enforcement staff are involved, that would be a different situation to consider. How serious the misbehavior is would determine what information goes on official school records.

The only thing parents like the Hightowers and Mr. Kline want is a variance. They won't accept the guilt of their son or daughter. They don't care what school staff tells them. They don't want a record of misbehavior to be on file. They fear some school employee – like a secretary who knows about the misbehavior – will begin a gossip chain.

Whenever a parent like Mr. Hightower says to a teacher or principal, "Do you know who I am?" the goal is quite clear. Mr. Hightower the Second and Mr. Kline are both demanding special treatment in the form of a variance. In some school districts, a Board of Education member may be persuaded to "punish" the principal or teacher instead of allowing the consequences to be applied immediately to the student. It is not uncommon for the rich, famous and powerful parents to get their child excused from a consequence. It is also not uncommon for a principal or teacher - who "hold their ground" and oppose a Board member's decision - to be told there will be a letter in *their* file. All school personnel know what that means. It means, in simple language, "Bug off. Don't make us look bad with parents who can make trouble for us – even take legal action. So don't do it again – or else."

Sad to say, the above is the truth. When school administrators and teachers are faced with a threat from a parent, a supervisor or a school board member, and they have evidence and truth on their side, they better find a good lawyer right away.

Seek a witness or two if at all possible. For example, Ms. Rodriguez's secretary would be a credible witness. One or two of Henry's teachers would be credible witnesses. Mr. Harvey might not have a witness to his conversation with Mr. Kline although he can take a photo of the carved desk and get a written statement from Suzanne's classroom teacher.

Above all else, when school districts develop school rules and post them on school walls, a copy of the rules should be mailed to the parents the first week of school. Consequences must appear next to each rule. What's more, all parents must sign the rules and consequences list and return them to the school office – SIGNED by the parent or parents or legal guardian. Parents who may not agree to one or two rules have the opportunity to meet with an administrator to discuss things. In the end, however, a signed rules and consequences list MUST be received for every student in the school. All we're asking/requiring is that parents are signing to indicate they read and understand the school rules and the consequences applied to broken rules.

Prevention is far less costly in time and effort than intervention which can cost school districts thousands – even a million - in time, effort, legal costs, reputations and heartache.

As we explored earlier, 'It's not fair!" Much of life isn't fair. For the sake of improving public schools and strengthening parent support, smart people have to do smart things. If you are a smart school leader yet you are not functioning as a smart leader, you do not belong in your elevated position.

Next page is **W** – four more to go

W

WITHDRAWAL

Our W word becomes the fourth and final one of the Goals of Misbehavior. Withdrawal is a sad sort of goal. In school, the student is not overtly seeking attention, demanding control or seeking revenge – at least at that time of his or her life. The child, the older student or adult has learned how to hide in quiet ways. They appear to be behaving, although they are misbehaving due to their refusal to accept either a challenge or help. They made a decision to kind of drop out after their needs were not met along the way. In all fairness, sometimes a person's needs are difficult for others in his or her life to meet. However, in many cases it appears the very young child may not have had sufficient early attention, belonging, caring and loving needs met. And so, Withdrawal is the goal she or he eventually chooses.

We have now reached the 23rd letter of the alphabet and named it **W** for Withdrawal. Your first question may be: How can a state of withdrawal be considered misbehavior? Here are just a few examples to consider. Each one is different yet the Four Goals of Misbehavior apply.

Marko was a child who entered kindergarten the day after his 5th birthday. His first few days of school found him getting into all kinds of mischief. He wandered around the room when the rest of the class was engaged in planned activities. He climbed on the tables and danced and acted silly. He threw crayons and scissors on the floor. After a week of annoyance and frustration for the teacher as well as Marco's classmates, I was asked to get involved. I checked on Marco's performance at kindergarten registration in March. At that time, our "readiness" team recommended Marco's parents delay his entrance to kindergarten – give him what we called the Gift of Time and enter kindergarten next year. Marco's mother agreed. His father did not. Dad wanted his boy in school.

When we met with Marco's mother, she expressed concern with his behavior at home. She said Marco was like another person since school began. Marco was starting to flush his 7 year old brother's toys down the toilet. He was also urinating on the floor in front of the toilet so that his mother would have to clean it up. He would cry when he was scolded and say he was sorry. His mother was clearly loving, caring and worried about Marco's sudden change in behavior.

It was clear to the teacher and me that Marco's misbehavior began with attention-getting. That behavior didn't get him what he wanted – to get out of this place where he knew he didn't yet belong. His misbehavior then progressed to Goal 2 and eventually to Goal 3 at home – revenge. Marco's misbehavior had a purpose and he was intelligent and determined enough to do whatever it took to get him out of school. This adorable little guy didn't belong there and he knew it.

Unfortunately, his father still wouldn't agree to letting Marco go home for the year and play indoors and outdoors, letting Mother Nature do the maturation job that would prepare him for strong readiness for kindergarten next year.

Marco's misbehavior continued during the second week of school. The teacher and I set up an after-school meeting with Marco's parents. His mother agreed. His father said he'd do his best to attend the meeting after work. Next afternoon, Marco played by himself with cars and trucks while the teacher, Marco's mother and I waited for Marco's dad to arrive. Dad was already a half-hour late. All students had left for the day as well as several teachers. I happened to look around to see why Marco was so quiet when I realized he wasn't in the room. I had an awful feeling that he had run out of the room without our seeing him. The teacher started looking in the hallway while Marco's mother stayed sitting where she was holding her three-month old baby. I asked where she had parked her car and what model it was. I'll never forget the look on her face. "I parked in front of the school and, oh my god, I left the motor running." I yelled, "Stay here" to her and ran through the halls (broke all rules) until I reached the front door. I saw the dark blue Chevy out front. The motor was running and Marco was in the driver's seat. The doors were locked! Marco's little hands were gripping the lower part of the steering wheel. It was almost impossible for him to actually drive the car since he couldn't even look out the windshield. Still, I was frantic. If the hand brake was not on, could he shift from Park to Drive? All four windows were up tight so I knocked on the driver's side window where a young five year old was trying to steer the car away from this place where he didn't belong. Marco looked up at me with teary eyes. As calm as I could become, I asked him to please unlock the door. He shook his head slowly back and forth. I felt helpless and no one was outside within shouting distance. I couldn't leave Marco and run for help. No cell phone in my pocket. I did what many of us do when a child is in danger and time is running out. I lied.

Through the driver's side window, I shouted for Marco to please look at me. He did. Then I told him that I had good news. His Daddy said he didn't have to go to kindergarten until he was six years old. Marco looked interested. He dropped his small hands from the steering wheel. I asked him to please press the lock. At that moment, I heard running feet coming in our direction. The teacher was first, followed by Marco's mother cradling the baby. I told Marco his mommy was coming to drive him home. Marco reached up and pressed the unlock button and all four locks popped up!

The emotions stay with me and, I suspect Marco's mother and teacher, even today. Marco has just graduated high school with honors. His future is looking great. Whenever I see Marco's mother at various school functions, we look at each other and smile, although we do not laugh. There was nothing funny about Marco's physical Withdrawal from school. The potential harm to Marco and others still makes my heart skip a beat.

Marco is a classic example of how the Four Goals of Misbehavior can work quickly, and in order. Marco's began one week as an attention-getter in his kindergarten class as well as at home. The second week he slipped into Control behavior, again, at home as well as at school. By the end of the second week, Marco had upped the ante and was into Goal 3 – Revenge. He became destructive at home – hurtful to his brother and mother. The Gift of Time was explored again with his mother, who was 100% behind it. His father rejected the recommendation. He feared we were suggesting his son was not intelligent and he wouldn't listen to our developmental explanation.

Finally, Marco's behavior deteriorated to the point where he just gave up. He withdrew from the kindergarten classroom and left the "scene." If the school halls had more people in them, someone would have seen a little boy fleeing, hurrying down the long sidewalk and entering the car. That did not happen.

Marco's father never showed up for the meeting but his excuse was plausible. He had a flat tire. His cell calls to his wife went unanswered because her purse was in the back seat of her car. Marco's father finally agreed to give his son the Gift of Time after he heard <u>part</u> of the story of Marco's own withdrawal from kindergarten. "Pretty smart kid I got, dontcha think?" was his first remark. As for his wife's accidentally leaving the unlocked car motor running at the curb and Marco's locking the car doors was the part never revealed to his father by the teacher or by me. If Marco's mother wanted to tell him, she was the one to do it.

I rarely ever saw a well-behaved child move so quickly from Goal 1, Goal 2, Goal 3 to Goal 4. It's more common for each misbehavior Goal to move downward over a longer period of time. My experience with Marco is something I'll never forget.

Mr. Stanton was the proud father of a baby girl, named Anita. After a week of Paternity Leave, he went back to school and into his 5th grade classroom. He was early and had plenty of time to prepare for the kids. He took a wrapped package from the bag and slipped it into his side desk drawer. That would have to stay there until just the right time.

Students loved Mr. Stanton and he loved them right back. Rarely did he have any serious misbehavior to deal with. He had taken a course during the summer that dealt with all the main points in this book. Class Rules and Consequences were prominently placed for all to see. He especially liked Doing the Unexpected – it was a fun thing for the class, as well. They got the message.

The one student who concerned Mr. Stanton the most was a boy named Josef. He saw Josef as one very angry dude. The school counselor told Mr. Stanton that Josef had been unhappy in foster care until a year ago. Now he was living with an older couple whose adult children lived on the west coast. The couple loved kids of all ages, especially those just entering kindergarten. Somehow, Josef's "story" moved the couple to tears and they asked to take a chance with a 10 year old. They did so at the beginning of his 5th grade year. They felt they were making some positive changes with Josef's anger and that he was feeling more like he belonged in their home. Now, his 5th grade school year was coming to an end. He missed Mr. Stanton when he was on Paternity Leave and didn't like the substitute one bit. He told the counselor a week later that Mr. Stanton was the best teacher he ever had.

Back to Mr. Stanton's first day back to school after a week at home with his wife and the baby. The first bell rang and the 5th graders were getting settled in their seats for opening exercises. Included were two girls and one boy telling the class what they ate for breakfast. Mr. Stanton was what the kids called "A nutritious breakfast freak." Since he considered that a compliment, he accepted the honor the kids had bestowed upon him. After applauding the three students' rendition of their morning nutritious breakfast, Mr. Stanton told them he had a surprise to show them. He went to the bottom drawer of his desk and pulled out that wrapped package. He unwrapped it and held it up for the students to see. It was an 8 x 10 photo of his baby girl. Her name *was Anita. The class erupted in applause. Mr. Stanton smiled from ear to ear. He told the class he was going to keep the photo on display all day. They could look at it but they could not touch it.*

When the class was quiet and ready for math, Mr. Stanton used a Power Point introduction to get started. Students had their computers open for use after the teacher's lesson. Mr. Stanton noticed Josef with his head down on the desk. He walked over to Josef and quietly asked him if he was feeling OK. Josef raised his head and yelled, "No, you SOB! Let me alone." Mr. Stanton said later that he was stunned and felt hurt at Josef's words and outburst. He remembered to do a 1 to 5 silent count, nod his head to Josef and walk back to the front of the room. He finished his Power Point presentation and then the class could do their math work on the computer. Mr. Stanton noticed Josef was just sitting there, staring into space. He was reluctant to approach him yet so he just walked around the room, monitoring the students' progress.

He heard someone walk through the room and approach his desk. Suddenly, Josef reached out his arm and swept the photo of Mr. Stanton's baby girl off the desk and onto the floor. The crash scared the class and then reality hit them when they saw who had done what. Mr. Stanton told everyone to stay where they were - to stay cool - that we'll work this out. He said he didn't have time to do the 1 to 5 silent count, mostly because he was in shock. He found his voice and said, as calmly as possible, "Josef, I'll need your help in cleaning up the glass. Stay where you are and I'll find a dust broom and pan." As Josef turned to flee, Mr. Stanley asked him again to" Stay put 'cause I'll need your help. Just give me thirty seconds in the closet."

Josef stood frozen beside the broken glass. When Mr. Stanton returned from his supply closet, he gave Josef the pan and broom while Mr. Stanton picked up the photo of the baby and laid it face-down on his desk. Josef did his best with the glass, although the small slivers would need the custodian to handle. Mr. Stanton asked a student to be in charge for five minutes. He knew who to pick. Then he took a chance and put his hand on Josef's shoulder and whispered, "You're not in trouble. Come on buddy, let's try to find Ms Jacobs."

Ten days later, Josef returned to class. What happened in his absence from school was not a miracle. Instead, it was the work of a teacher who cared for and about all his students and a counselor who understood goals of misbehavior and didn't overreact. The counselor told Mr. Stanton how Josef totally broke down in her office. She said he cried and cried to the point where she called a doctor. The doctor recommended he see a therapist whose reputation was sterling. His foster parents were supportive and did everything they were asked to do. Josef had reached rock bottom - which is Goal 4 or Withdrawal. Mr. Stanton met with Josef twice before the 5th grader could go back to school. They discussed how to handle his return. Mr. Stanton asked if Josef would consider telling his classmates the reason he damaged the photo frame. Josef had to think awhile before agreeing to do that.

On that 10th day back to school, Josef stood up in front of his classmates and apologized. He made a special apology to his teacher. Then he explained his behavior/misbehavior. He told them that when he saw the picture of the baby, it reminded him that he has no pictures of himself as a baby. He wished he knew what he had looked like.

"The only picture I had of me was my first grade school picture. And I look dorky on that one. I've been in foster care almost my whole life. If there are any pictures, they probably got lost when I moved from one family to another. When I saw that cute baby on the picture, it made me wonder how I looked when I was born."

As he sat down at his desk, Josef received something he never before had – a standing ovation. His teacher walked over and gave him a quick hug.

Josef had to pay Mr. Stanton for the broken picture frame. He paid with two hours' work in the classroom – after school - doing some cleaning and organizing, as well as helping to prepare for a science project.

Josef is an example of a child who moved from Goal 1 misbehavior to Goal 2 misbehavior. Neither Goal was working for him. When he saw that baby picture, he dropped instantly to Goal 3 or Revenge. He had to hurt somebody – and he did. Fortunately the person he hurt understood what it was like to be Josef. With assistance from the counselor, Mr. Stanton knew just what to do.

Ted was an adult before he reached the Goal of Revenge. In fact, he had achieved great accomplishments in science and mathematics throughout his public schooling and entered Harvard at age 20. His IQ was very, very high. Ted was blessed with loving and caring parents as well as his nice, caring brother. He overcame a serious medical issue with hives when he was 6 months old and had to spend most of the next 8 months in isolation. In elementary school, his IQ was declared too high for 5th grade by school personnel so they advanced him to 7th grade. Ted himself feels that was a major reason for his later social/ emotional problems. He said he didn't fit in with the older kids and was bullied. Otherwise, his physical health seemed fine as he moved rapidly from college to teaching in college and universities during his 20's. He then became part of what was called a personality study at Harvard, although the study turned out to be a brutal psychological study, instead. The results were one of Ted's reasons for hating a system that didn't work for him.

Brilliant is the best word to describe his intelligence. However, he kept working in a field that didn't bring him happiness. He tried his best and his family always demonstrated their caring and commitment to his well-being. Ted wasn't much of a social creature and eventually decided he wanted to live in seclusion in nature. He thought he could be happy there. He was fascinated with nature and studied survival skills. Here are his words, words that moved his misbehavior from Goal 2 to Goal 3. He was then about 36 and had discovered one of his favorite nature areas – about a two-day hike from where he lived. He loved to go there. Perhaps he even found happiness in that environment.

Then the worst thing happened to him.

As a result, he began learning how to build his first bomb.

Ted's own words can be found in a lengthy Wikipedia article. Here they are.

"The best place, to me, was the largest remnant of this plateau that dates from the tertiary age. It's kind of rolling country, not flat, and when you get to the edge of it you find these ravines that cut very steeply

in to cliff-like drop-offs and there was even a waterfall there. It was about a two days' hike from my cabin. That was the best spot until the summer of 1983. That summer there were too many people around my cabin so I decided I needed some peace. I went back to the plateau and when I got there I found they had put a road right through the middle of it. You just can't imagine how upset I was. It was from that point on I decided that, rather than trying to acquire further wilderness skills, I would work on getting back at the system. Revenge."

Ted moved fully from the goal of Withdrawal and finally got his revenge.

He told us in his own words.

We know Ted as the Unabomber. For a lengthy, well-written article, go to https://en.wikipedia.org/wiki/Ted_Kaczynski

The above three examples show how the Goal of Withdrawal can be reached quickly or over time. Sometimes an individual who reaches Withdrawal has thoughts of suicide yet never attempts it. Sometimes individuals who reach Withdrawal actually take their own life. And sometimes individuals who feel life or "the system" have betrayed them time and again, while in their Withdrawal behavior, some plot to get even – seek revenge. In our society, we seem to be seeing a growing number of younger people who want to punish those who bully them or won't allow them to fit or belong in ways they want to fit or belong. In essence, they are saying,"I'll show them. They'll be sorry."

The suicide rate appears to be climbing for teens who live in a state of Withdrawal. Some experts are claiming the internet is responsible – that social media itself is misbehaving. Of course social media has no heart or feelings, although it does put human beings together in social units or groupings. As such, there are those who suggest that social media is partly responsible for the surge in teenage suicide – that accepting some joiners and not others – or for dropping access to former joiners - encourages thoughts of ending the lives of those most vulnerable. People in Goal 4 feel they don't belong where they want to belong.

Withdrawal is a goal where some find themselves after all other goals have failed for them. Withdrawal can be many things to those who seek it. Drugs, both prescription and illegal, can be involved. Some find Withdrawal a shelter and comfort while focusing on what they see as a terrible situation. Others go there to think about ending their life. Still others go there because they don't want to put any more effort into trying to belong or fit in – or be wanted. And others seek Withdrawal in order to plan revenge against someone or some group in order to get even for a real or even imagined rejection or betrayal. On the other hand, some suicide bombers will not commit suicide until they have reached the goal of revenge. Sometimes they live in isolation for years before they find the right time and place to seek their revenge. Think about that in light of what is happening today. Read David Ignatius' books for an eye-opener. People who withdraw due to dissatisfaction with their life are growing in numbers. They either remain in withdrawal or they remain there until they discover an opportunity to seek revenge. Either way, we cannot take this growing trend lightly.

Suicide or thoughts of suicide are forms of misbehavior. Others don't accept that premise. I wrestled with that same thinking. However, it could be the logic that sees suicide as taking a person's life. As such, killing is misbehavior, even if the person you kill is yourself. Consider, also, how often suicide is either attempted or carried out in order to "get even" with someone? Words are written on suicide notes that tend to include, "She'll be sorry now," or "He'll wish he never left me." More recently, manifestos are prepared before the suicide which describe either perceived or real geopolitical or cultural reasons why some people must die.

While it may seem that the Four Goals of Misbehavior are designed exclusively to assist teachers in their daily contact with kids, the Goals apply to any person of any age, type of employment or retirement. Remember Jake's grandma? She was in Goals 1 and 2. Remember Ted? It took him a long time to move through Goals 1 and 2 before he reached Goal 3 and then Goal 4, and then back to Goal 3 or the Revenge Goal. Remember Josef? He went to Goal 3 when he reached the teacher's desk and then plunged to Goal 4 after he realized the sad effect his misbehavior had on Mr. Stanton. There is hope for Josef, especially if his foster parents continue to give him that sense of belonging and are consistent in their caring relationship with him.

Dealing with misbehavior in your daily life – and especially in a career that deals with children of all ages – is difficult, to say the least. However, every kind of leader deals with a ladder that enables those under him or her to keep climbing for the leader's position. It happens all the time. Leaders not only lead others, they also deal with fending off those who would have the leader's job . Lots of misbehavin' going on.

Misbehavior as a human activity never rests and never ends. In school, when Rules and Consequences are posted the first day or two of school, the student behavior framework has been set. We must give children and teens more responsibility for their misbehavior. We talk too much to those misbehaving. We show our frustration and anger to those misbehaving. We take on too much of the responsibility in dealing with misbehavior than we should. Let's put more behavior control responsibility on the *individual* – the child, the teen-ager, the ladder-climbers, the old folks whose memories are still sharp enough to outwit family members and caretakers. Talk less. Expect more of those who create misbehavior problems in the first place.

The Four Goals of Misbehavior, as well as Rules where Consequences are applied *consistently*, can assist you every day.

On to **X-IT OUT**

X

X – IT OUT

We have finally reached the Final Four. As a big college basketball fan, I like using basketball terms for the Four Goals of Misbehavior. The Final Four in basketball is a worthy goal to reach just as the Four Goals of Misbehavior are important to learn, understand and use.

For umpteen years, parents, teachers and others who deal with misbehavin' children and adults came up with a hundred reasons or causes for an individual's misbehavior. What a waste of time. Let's blow the whistle right now. Too often, the misbehaving person wins and those of us in charge lose. Too often, we begin with one word – WHY? – and then embellish it with a few more.

Why did you do that? Response is, " I dunno"

I'll ask you just one more time. Why did you do that? "And I told you, I dunno."

Yes you do know. "It wasn't me. It was Carlos."

It was not Carlos. Carlos was absent today. "Oh, is he sick or something?"

I don't know why Carlos was absent. "Well, then I guess it wasn't him."

You can see what's happening here. Misbehavin' people – especially children and teens – are experts at taking the ball right out of our hands and dribbling down the floor in a different direction.

Kids are especially good at changing the subject, keeping the adult in charge floundering, making a U-turn and forcing the adult in charge to go out of bounds which puts the ball right back in the hands of the one misbehaving.

As adults in charge, our first question should not be Why?

Our first question to ourselves, in silence, should be "What's he after?"

Sometimes there is in me a need to semi-misbehave so let's X- out the following:

A ONE-SIZE FITS ALL KINDERGARTEN TO 12TH GRADE CURRICULUM

SCHOOL DISTRICTS THAT DON'T RESPECT EARLY CHILDHOOD EDUCATION

PARENTS WHO WANT EARLY ADMISSION FOR THEIR YOUNG FIVE YEAR OLD

PARENTS WHO ARE NOT SURE THEY REALLY WANTED CHILDREN

ADULTS WHO TALK TOO MUCH AND DO TOO LITTLE GOOD

TEENS WHO WEAR BEACH CLOTHES TO SCHOOL

ADULTS WHO DO NOT ACKNOWLEDGE HOMELESS PEOPLE ON THE STREET

BULLIES

GANGS

THE F-WORD COMING FROM PROFESSIONAL ATHLETES AND CELEBRITIES

Carol M. Hoffman, EdD

~~THE F-WORD COMING FROM ATHLETIC COACHES AND MANAGERS~~

~~LEADERS IN GOVERNMENT AND SCHOOLS WHO DO NOT CARE ENOUGH~~

~~CAREGIVERS OF THE YOUNGEST AND OLDEST WHO DO NOT CARE ENOUGH~~

~~ADULTS WHO DO NOT UNDERSTAND THE VALUE OF RULES & CONSEQUENCES~~

~~BUYING THINGS WE DON'T NEED WITH MONEY WE DON'T HAVE~~

~~REVEALING FAVORITES AMONG CHILDREN AND STUDENTS~~

~~WITNESSING CHILD ABUSE AND SAYING "I CAN'T DO ANYTHING ABOUT IT"~~

~~PEDOFILES~~

~~DOING FOR OTHERS WHO ARE ABLE TO DO THINGS FOR THEMSELVES~~

~~FORGETTING TO LOOK IN A MIRROR, SMILE & KNOW THAT YOU MATTER~~

ON TO **Y** AND **Z**

Y AND Z

YOU & ZEST

You are the only person you really know. You know yourself better than anyone else in the whole world. Like most people, you keep much of who you are to yourself. You have secrets you'll never reveal to anyone. You believe you are a good human being, yet you'd like to be an even better human being. Get rid of some of the flaws only you truly know exist. You'd also like to help your partner or your children or a friend to improve in some area of their personality or behavior.

If you see a need to change something about someone else – stop right now. It will be a waste of time and effort. On the other hand, if you see a need to change something about yourself, there's only one person who can do the job – YOU. If this is true – and I believe it is – then why do people spend so much of their time, effort and money on trying to change somebody else? If you are a teacher, you are trying to change a kid named Maureen or Jose or Tonya or Tyler or Heidi or Rasheed or Hunter. Every year you consider at least 25% of your class either incorrigible, lazy, rude, selfish or disinterested in learning.

If you are a parent, you are trying to change at least two of the following: your second child, your husband (or wife), your pet dog, your pet cat or your mother-in-law. Well, forget it. Just like the school teacher, you can't change anyone but yourself.

If you are a leader in a big business or a leader in an elected position, you work at trying to change others instead of yourself. You know better, of course, but there is that damned Junior Executive just drooling for your job. Or there is a new guy in town who wants to be Mayor instead of you and he's better looking and has the cash to beat you. Well, whether you are in a business or in the People's Business you can't change anything about your competition. All you can do is change something about yourself.

Conjure up some zest – some relish – and find more zest in your life.

If you have a zest for living, you *can* change for the better. If you talk too much, talk less. You'll live. You don't have to be Everything to Everybody. Put someone else in charge. If you always have to be right and never wrong, try to figure out the reason. It really is less stressful when you allow yourself to accept a badge of imperfection. Wear it proudly on your chest - or make a T-shirt that reads IMPERFECT AND GLAD OF IT. Just the laughs you'd get would ease your stress.

When people have zest in their life, they do not give others permission to say things that make them feel bad. They become truthful and brave and calm and say, "I did not give you permission to hurt my feelings," or "I'll let you know when I give you permission to say what you just said. And by the way, it may be a long wait." Then back out of that conversation so you don't end up in a confrontation. Turn and walk away swiftly with your head held high, a spring in your step and out of that person's space.

Put some zest into your life.

Let's meet a man who combined brilliance and knowledge with joy and zest. Add caring and a sense of humor and you just met Heinz Ansbacher. I met Dr. Ansbacher one summer at a university in New England. He was teaching a weekend course and three of us from my school district were lucky enough to be accepted. Our Superintendent, our Reading Supervisor and I made up our group. The Superintendent's attendance demonstrates his commitment to a school-wide emphasis on Adlerian psychology. We knew Dr. Ansbacher from afar – through his work with Alfred Adler. An article in the *New York Times* on June 24, 2006 included the following. "Over

30 years ago, Dr. Ansbacher wrote a trilogy in collaboration with his wife, Dr. Rowena Ansbacher, in which they analyzed and commented on Adler's works. The books were widely regarded as indispensable in the fields of individual and abnormal psychology."

The course was indispensable to our school district's curriculum, teachers, principals, counselors, nurses, bus drivers, cafeteria staff and others who interacted with kids of all ages. We were determined to apply Adler's and Dreikurs' work in helping students develop self-discipline and cooperation with others. We were especially determined to help teachers learn how to defuse and resolve misbehavior problems, develop class rules and consequences and deal more effectively in all areas where potential problems tend to emerge. And, of course, encourage staff to talk less and accomplish more.

The morning of our second day's class was devoted to Early Recollections. Dr. Ansbacher gave each person in the course a large file card. In his special way – with eyes twinkling and a big smile on his face – he told us he didn't want us to write a book. That's why he gave all of us the same kind of writing paper. Another reason for the file card was to maintain confidentiality – he wanted no names on the file card. He preferred printing and made sure we all received the pencils he provided. No pens. He wanted no clues as to the writer. And then he got us ready. He said,

"I want you to sit back and relax in those hard chairs. Ah, you are looking relaxed already. What a bright bunch you are. Ah, now you are really relaxed so this is what I want you to do. I want you to go back in time – in your mind, of course. Close you eyes if you want. No need to, though. Do it your way. Do not be in a hurry to write. Think first. Keep going back as far as you can – put your brain in, what's it called? Rewind! When you have a vivid memory of a time in your early childhood, begin printing about it. Begin with, 'I am ....and then stay in the moment of that time. Talk of colors if you remember them. Who are the people and the place where you are – or are you all by yourself?"

Then Dr. Ansbacher gave us an example, which was helpful. He asked if anyone needed more help and no one indicated they did.

"I will ask no one to leave the room while others are still writing.

Those speedy ones who finish first will just put their pencil down over the paper and wait until the entire class is finished. Understood? Oh. Yes. If you do not want me to read your early recollection to the class, you must tell me before we return for the afternoon.

We were amazed at how we felt during the whole process. The way Dr. Ansbacher prepared us for the activity is the way classroom teachers should prepare their students for special activities or expectations. We were also amazed at how relaxed we felt as we went back in our mind to retrieve a long-ago memory. Everyone who finished early followed the rules. No one spoke or left the room until Dr. Ansbacher quietly announced that everyone was finished. He collected all the cards without looking at them and also asked a student to shuffle them "really good – like a what do you call them in Las Vegas? Oh, yes. A card shark." And then he laughed at his joke. His wife of about 60 years smiled her adoring smile at her long-time husband and co-author. They were always together. What a treat for those of us in that classroom in New England.

After lunch, we all gathered back in the classroom, in anticipation of what was to come next. Dr. Ansbacher said he read every file card and found them all interesting. Then he laughed. "And some were *very* interesting." Then we all laughed – that nervous laugh of people who wondered what their early recollection meant to the professor.

He told us he would read a few. "I'll read even more if we have time. After I read each memory, I will tell you how I think you turned out – what you are like today just by the memory you chose as well as why you chose it. Do not reveal yourself to me. Stay a mystery! If you want to talk to me at a later time, call me. My phone number is in the directory. By now in your lives, you have hundreds of thousands of memories stored in your brain. Millions, perhaps. Most of you like to remember – we all have favorite memories – yet some of our memories will remain hidden, either by conscious choice or by just......sort of like forgetting them. Your very early ones – we call Early Recollections – are particularly important to know about, especially if you are having a serious problem right now in your life. Those early memories are very enlightening to the counselor or doctor you may be seeing for help.

With that, Dr. Ansbacher shuffled the file cards once again, fanned them out and then chose the first one he would read.

Exploring Early Recollections is not a parlor game. It, also, is not fortune telling. Unless you have more knowledge and skills using Early Recollections within a group, please do not attempt to "guess at" what those remembrances mean. However, you may already know enough about ER to ask friends or family members to write down the earliest recollection they want to choose among their remembrances. They may wish to share theirs or not. Never insist they must share it with others. Sometimes it's just personally fascinating or interesting for an individual to think about the reason she or he remembered that particular ER. Whatever you do, follow Dr. Ansbacher's precise and essential "lead up" instructions offered above.

If you find Dr. Ansbacher's written work useful and worthy of reading, check out Amazon, Adler University in Chicago or university book stores in the US. My opinion of him and the three works he and his wife, Rowena translated from Adler's German writing is over the top. Dr. Ansbacher became a student of Adler and, eventually, a colleague. They worked together for almost ten years before Adler's death. Both contributed significantly to a practical, commonsense view of people as social creatures needing to belong and to feel important.

That human being, Heinz Ansbacher, was full of zest until his death in 2006 at the age of 101.

Webster's New World Dictionary defines zest as *Something that gives flavor or relish; a stimulating quality; keen enjoyment such as a zest for life*. I suspect Dr. Ansbacher would be delighted to be described as *relish*.

I'll offer Dr. Ansbacher's interpretation of my Early Recollection before we reach the next section. It was the third file card he chose. Here it is.

I am five years old and in kindergarten. Even though it was a windy day, Miss Kegerise took the class outside for fresh air. After we played ball on the grass and hopscotch on the macadam, we lined up to go back inside. The kindergarten class was at the back of the building – and access to our class was at least 15 wide steps to climb. I never understood why little kids were located in the worst possible location. Anyway, Miss Kegerise asked me to hold the door open for everyone. The wind was really fierce, so she told me to hold tight when I opened the door. I climbed those steps first, reached the old kind of double door with brass bars, pulled it open and the door blew open so far that I was hanging over an almost 20 foot drop onto concrete that led to the cellar door. Miss Kegerise yelled for me to hang on. She would get Mr. Brady to help. She also told the other children to stay where they were but to sit down because the wind had become fierce. I was swinging in the wind over that far drop and trying to be brave. But I was scared. I knew enough not to look down which would scare me more! Finally, the janitor (now called a custodian) arrived and came to rescue me. He kept telling me to hold tight and not let go of the bar on the door. I don't remember exactly how he got me off the brass bar. I think he yanked the whole door towards him so I'd be back on the top step. That way, I could let go and be on safe ground. Miss Kegerise came to hug me. She said she thought she was more scared than I was. That made me smile. She promised to send a note home for my mom so she'd know what happened. (On the housing project we had no phone in our apartments – only a phone booth at the end of the street) I'll remember that day – and FEEL the emotions – for as long as I live.

As Dr. Ansbacher read my ER, I remember sitting like a statue, not wanting to give away that he was reading my file card. He read a few more after mine, although I don't remember those. I was too stunned.

This was Dr. Ansbacher's assessment of my ER. *This person is an administrator – in either the medical field or the field of education. He or she – I think a she because her printing is so neat. Men, nah, don't write so good as women. (he laughs) This person loves children and she wants to save them – that is – she wants to be what Americans call an advocate – that is she wants to take care of them. She is also a cautious person – yah – that is she is always thinking of safety for others. Maybe she isn't thinking so much of her own safety – she might even be a bit – what would you call it? Yah, a bit of a rebel. A risk taker – that's it! A risk-taker. Remember, she survived a dangerous situation! She remembers surviving. Yes! That's it. She's also a survivor. She loves to live. She has children of her own – maybe many of them."*

What a remarkable experience for me. Whether or not everything Dr. Ansbacher said was accurate or true, his assessment hit home. However, I do not see myself as a risk-taker, although I never met a challenge I didn't set out to meet. I kept thinking, how could my early recollection tell him so much? Once my three-days of classes with Dr. Ansbacher ended, I felt I was going home with many gifts – gifts that would carry me through hard times and good times in public education.

On to Beyond A to Z

BEYOND A TO Z

FINAL LOOK AT THE FOUR GOALS OF MISBEHAVIOR

Here's a final look at the **Four Goals of Misbehavior** – kind of a booster shot. You may feel you don't quite grasp the concepts. Most of us still think of *causes* of misbehavior instead of silently asking ourselves, "What is he after?" We can fit what he wants in one of four goals. He's either after attention, control, revenge or withdrawal. When you think *causes*, your list to check them out can run to 100 or more. Why give yourselves more work and frustration?

The Four Goals of Misbehavior can be helpful to teachers, parents and others who deal with children on a regular basis. Remember, older adults can also fit these four categories.

The suggestions below are just examples of things you can say to the misbehaving person. They are not in any way the ONLY way to respond. Phrases and responses similar to the examples below are just a few of the many you could come up with and use with success.

Goal 1 Attention – children who need to be noticed; they are annoying and disruptive; some can't get enough laughs. (remember Cassandra?) *Give attention when person is not demanding it. This is the busiest yet least serious goal; however disruptive attention-seekers must follow rules and accept consequences at school and at home. Same goes for adults who seek excessive attention.*

Goal 2 Control or Power - behavior that makes us angry; child or adult challenges our authority or control over others and situations;

person needs to be in charge all the time. Sometimes is a bully with a reputation. Argues, threatens. Tempts adult to lose control. *Avoid losing control! Do not move into the person's space; keep a distance, say something like "I haven't decided what to do about this. For now, let's stay away from one another" and slowly back away. Look interested in the wall clock or your watch and get back to what you were doing. Deal with problem later unless the one misbehaving seems ready to mend things now. Loss of control over others and situations is so vivid in professional athletes. If they believe an opposition player has "wronged" them, they will show anger in different ways – none of them considered positive behavior. If they don't "overcome" the wrong immediately, real or imagined, they will wait for their chance – if not now, later - with later being in the next game. Now those players are ready to rumble. They have reached Goal 3 – Revenge.*

Goal 3 Revenge - behavior that stuns or shocks you; makes you feel hurt, even betrayed, devastated. Misbehavior is serious and could be dangerous to you or others around you. Person is "getting even" for something he/she believes was your fault. *The athletes mentioned above "get even" in different ways, depending on the type of sport they are playing. Baseball pitchers aim for the head or other body part of a batter. Football players make illegal tackles or face mask assaults. NBA players trip opponents or grab them around the neck and other fouls that are determined by the referees as Intentional Fouls. On the other hand, Revenge often "waits" years to emerge; remember Ted? In Ted's case, his target person was never near him; instead his revenge took place via mail. Remember the student, Josef, and his sudden move into revenge? His target – Mr. Stanton – had no personal fear of Josef. He did his count to 5 and stayed calm so he could deal immediately with the situation in Josef's space. Typically,at the moment of revengeful behavior, attempt to stay cool and, if safe, engage the person by asking, "What was your reason for doing this?" Attempt to get person engaged while also asking for help via phone. Let misbehaving person see you as "cool" yet* *making a plan. If misbehavior is dangerous to you, physically, get away and seek help. Sometimes no matter what you do, there is no escape from a revengeful person.*

Goal 4 Withdrawal – *person prefers to be alone; his/her behavior makes us feel helpless; child won't allow us to help in school or open up at home with parents. Quietly refuses to accept the challenges of everyday life; may see life as not worth living. Can be depression or at least severe unhappiness. Seek counseling help and parental help. Could be drug or alcohol issue but not always. Suicidal thoughts may be involved.*

In all Four Goals of Misbehavior, the child/student/adult does not feel a sense of belonging in his or her social group. A family is a somewhat small social group. A school has a number of social groups made from a large population. A church or place of worship is a spiritual social group. These days, Face Book is a popular social outlet for kids and adults. A gang is a social group. There are others, of course. The importance of believing in and using the Four Goals of Misbehavior is huge. Begin the school year - or calendar year at home - by developing 4 or 5 rules and logical consequences for breaking a rule. The students are involved with the teacher being the one to make the final list and post it where all can see it. For kids at home, the parents are the ones to make the final list and post it on the refrigerator. Once the rules are established and the teacher or parent becomes savvy with the Four Goals of Misbehavior, the teacher or parent and the kids create a social group where everyone belongs and fits in. No one is allowed to be a total comedian or a total bossy kid or a "get-even" kid or a total loner. Personalities differ but respect and caring about others must thrive.

Together, The Four Goals of Misbehavior represent the best clue to the misbehavior occurring at any given moment in time. People like me believe that – as Adler, Dreikurs, Ansbacher and their followers discovered – neither good behavior nor misbehavior are accidental.

Good behavior and misbehavior have a social purpose. Misbehavior doesn't just happen. It is not accidental, although many individuals engaged in misbehavior would like us to believe that fairy tale. There is a purpose and it's the job of the one in charge to find out which of the Four Goals the individual is after.

Will your use of ignoring Goal 1 pests always work? Of course not. Most of the time, it will. You'll learn creative ways, especially with the early childhood years, to ask the child before she does her class clown routine, "Angie, how many times do you think you'll need to have extra attention today? Four? Three? Which do you think it is? (Truly believe this – Angie will say "four" which will be seven or eight times less than she interrupts now). Give Angie four green paper circles. They are hers to give back to you as she moves through four interruptions. Once she uses up all four, give her a red paper circle. That means "no more or expect consequences." You'll be surprised that after a few days, Angie might ask for three green circles. She will know, in advance, that the consequence of going beyond her green circles means Time out – or whatever other logical consequence is determined, in advance. Teacher handles this situation without missing a beat during a lesson. Teacher talk-time is reduced during the procedure. Teacher's goal is to get Angie down to one or two disruptions a day.

When you get really good at identifying which goal is at work in another person, you won't have to pause as much to silently figure it all out. Once you figure it out, your verbal and nonverbal responses will come to you pretty quickly. Eventually, you won't even ask, "WHY did you do that?" Eventually, you will see that your relationship with others will become less problematic and more enjoyable.

The key is this: You have to **want** to improve your relationship with others, young and old. If you are motivated enough to become a more effective, caring and successful teacher or parent or daughter-in-law or caretaker or business leader, then determine to make changes in the way you behave. All of us are capable of getting better and better and better from this day forward.

As one teacher likes to say to her colleagues, "You HaftaWanta."

The Four Goals of Misbehavior will make more sense as we continue exploring the concept. When the Goals are understood and applied, they can and will defuse a potentially serious flare-up. Think of it this way. Picture a stick of dynamite with the fuse attached at one end. In school, a child holds a match to the end of the fuse. At home, a child or a misbehaving adult holds the match to the end of the fuse. And at work, an adult holds a match to the end of the fuse. The adult who does not want the flame to reach the end of the fuse and experience a big explosion gets out an imaginary scissors and cuts the fuse so the flame disappears. How can adults defuse nasty flare-ups, especially in a group setting like school? Following are a few ideas when you want to defuse a potential flare-up so that you can keep moving on a track you have begun and want to finish without interruption.

A Silent count to 5
Remain calm
Make eye contact. Remain serious. Say, "We gotta work this out at a later time. Let's pick a time. We can't let this hurt our friendship (or relationship)
Move on, resolve later privately.

Say, "I'm feeling bad that you're feeling bad. How about a hug? Let's talk about it later. " (for younger kids)
Move on, talk about it later, privately.

Say, "Right now I am so ticked off I don't know what to do. Until I *do* know what to do, please stay ten feet away from me."
Move on, resolve later privately.

Say, "Did I give you permission to say that?" Wait for a "no." "Then unless I give you permission you will not say that again."
Move on. Problem may already be resolved.

Sing Glocca Morra like Gwen sang it. Or pick a different song – maybe Ain't Misbehavin' or Cry Me a River or your own creative choice. You don't need a professional singing voice – just belt out the song and then............

Take a bow and move on.

Say, "Did you do that to help or to hurt?" Wait for response, which is likely "to help." Then ask, "How does it help?" Response is likely a shrug or an "I don't know." Then say, "Then tell me about it later. In the meantime, both of you stay away from each other." Move on.

Work it out later. It's unlikely a person would admit they "did that to hurt someone."

Say, "Did you get what you wanted when you did that?"

Work it out according to the answer.

Pledge Allegiance to the flag – I used that when two kindergartners were annoying me or interrupting a lesson by constantly tattling on each other – pain in the butt kind of annoyance - nothing serious. I spoke no words, turned toward the flag, put my hand over my heart and recited the Pledge – they usually did the Pledge, as well - then I pointed to an activity area and they got the message. I refused to respond to chronic tattling from that day on – unless there was a serious dispute that needed intervention. My teacher colleagues claimed my kindergartners were the most patriotic kids in the school.

Do the Unexpected – be creative – put a little zest in your life's work.

One main focus throughout the book was on The Four Goals of Misbehavior as they apply to the challenging misbehavior of children in a family, students in school, young children in day care, relatives, co-workers, and other adults who live and work in our communities and our world. Some readers may find it hard to believe that any kind of misbehavior can be either identified and resolved with just four goals or defused for the time being. Defusing is a way of "buying time" so you can deal with an issue later, when all parties have cooled down.

Misbehavior is never accidental. All behavior has a purpose. When you see misbehavior coming your way, silently ask yourself, "What's he after when he does that?" He's either after attention, control, revenge or withdrawal.

MEMORY AND EARLY RECOLLECTIONS

Memory

Let's begin with Memory. All people in the world are living longer than ever before – at least history suggests this. We do know that in the United States alone, women and men who can either count on longevity through genetics or those who maintain a healthy weight and avoid drug and alcohol abuse, are living well into their 90s. How many of those living into their 90s – even reaching 100 – are living happy healthy lives? Some are, of course, and many are not.

At least two memory issues facing older people today are Dementia and Alzheimer's. Had people who lived in past times lived as long as people live today, those two memory issues may not have reached the large numbers we see today. Scientific and Medical advances have increased our chance to reach a ripe old age, yet they haven't found out how to cure aging brain diseases.

Scientists and doctors are discovering ways that may delay Dementia and, perhaps slow the progression of Alzheimer's, although not cure them. We already know that many adult children are becoming caretakers for their aging parents afflicted with some sort of physical and/or memory issue or disease. Those caretakers are becoming our national heroes. They need not only our praise but our help, as well. Some communities are developing Adult Day Care centers in order to give family caretakers much-needed breaks. Other communities are offering group sessions for the family caretakers – giving advice, ideas and a feeling of belonging to others in their situation and in their present challenging lives. It takes more energy than most of us have to make it through those rough caretaker days and nights. Children aren't the only human beings in need of feeling they belong – or that they fit in – with others.

Adults with memory issues caring for other adults with memory issues is a potentially challenging situation. This is where serious misbehavior can come in. I know adults in their 60s who are experiencing some memory issues while also caring for parents in their 80s who have serious memory issues. Imagine the frustrations that can lead to misbehavior on the part of individuals at either end. We will undoubtedly see different types of misbehavior in elder care growing in numbers over the next ten years. Are we ready to respond in preventative ways?

Consider this: Human beings may have just three life pathways. Thoughts, Experiences and Memories

Misbehavior can and will occur as we travel those pathways. And so, the pathway to memory has to be part of our explorations into misbehavior. There are so many ways we can misbehave as we travel through life, trying to belong and to fit.

A PERSONAL JOURNEY WITH MILD MEMORY CHALLENGES

All my adult life, I always knew a person's name instantly whenever and wherever I saw him or her. In my many years of work in public schools, I remembered everybody – kids as well as adults. Then about two years' ago, I experienced the first time I couldn't name a baseball player I've followed for years. I went through the alphabet, A to Z, *twice* – I eventually recalled his name - Cal Ripkin. I said his name three more times to myself. A few weeks later, I could recall his name and say it without hesitation. As time went on, I occasionally had to do the A to Z thing – annoying as it was – and eventually I'd recall and say the name. Then that experiment needed a boost so I added a picture of the person in my mind – and that helped for awhile.

I didn't then, nor do I now have a terrible memory problem. I write letters, e-mail and books and do everything else I do with my brain every day. However, I was trying to come up with a more efficient way to remember occasional names or objects. I mention objects now because when I couldn't remember the word *lattice* – even when I could picture that big white yard thing that hung on the walls of Lowe's store – the name wouldn't come to me. I bought a fifty-cent notebook and had an idea what to do with it. I made two columns on a page. On the left column, I wrote the word WORD. On the right column, I wrote the word or words that became my MNEMONIC. (don't pronounce the M unless you can!).

My memory of names and objects improved from that day on.

Lattice was my first word in the left Word or Object column of my notebook. Under the right Mnemonic heading, I wrote the word *lettuce*. For more than a year, I've had no need to check my notebook when I see lattice (or even lettuce) in someone's garden. The word comes to me right away.

Cal Ripkin's name is now remembered almost instantly when I am discussing his amazing record in baseball. My Mnemonic for Cal Ripkin is "rips the ball." I recall the mnemonic which retrieves Cal's name. My most recent need for a mnemonic was when I was discussing the Mets with my son, Tod. I couldn't remember the left field player's name yet I remembered he had played earlier with the San Francisco Giants. My son quickly told me, " His name is Matt Kemp." My son also remembered that Matt Kemp lives in an eleven million dollar house! I won't forget that number. Back to his name. I knew I would have to put Kemp's name in my notebook for future help. The mnemonic I came up with was "a mat of hemp."

Yes, I know you are ready to call the Goon Squad to pick me up. However, since I listed the names/objects and mnemoic in the notebook, I have not had to refer to any of those 38 words. My old brain has decided to go with the mnemonics, no matter how strange it seems. I promise you this works for me.

My purpose in describing this experience is not so you think I have made a significant brain/memory discovery. I have not – and I know it. Still, it is a discovery that helps me. If the idea helps others, that would make me happy for them. Mostly, I am just determined and will not give in to lapses when remembering names and objects. Going through the alphabet a few times still works for me occasionally, although that method takes too much time for me to recover that name or word. By using a mnemonic that is personal to me, I can get a quick recovery. If you decide to give this method a try, your mnemonics have to be personal to you. Also, you need to know that there are a few obscure names I couldn't quickly remember throughout one year. I just chose not to add them to my notebook. They weren't important for me to remember.

Here is a sample of the two-column list I made in my fifty-cent notebook. These samples could be useful to anyone who wants to retain words that are personally important for them to remember.

Notebook begun on 6/15/16

People's names or Objects	Mnemonics
Lattice	lettuce
Jason Werth	worth millions
Deductible	de duck
Dr. Haines	Dr. Stockings
Dianthus	Diana
Cal Ripkin	rips the ball
Maple tree	syrup
Michael Jordan	Old Man River
Matt Kemp	a mat of hemp
Circuit breaker	break the circus
Paul Newman	Newman from Seinfeld
Bryce Harper	Harper Valley PTA

In one year, I wrote down 38 names or objects I had trouble remembering – and was determined to remember. The above are just examples from those 38. I paired each with a word or words that held a personal clue as to the name or object I couldn't readily recall. Sounds a tad weird to me that in order to release the word my brain wants to keep, I have to provide a kind of link made up of several words. I'm baffled by having several words help my brain release just one word. So far, however, that system is working well for me. How long will it work? Only time will tell. In the meantime, I feel happy with the results. As I say the "link word or phrase," the name I couldn't remember comes to me right away. My old method of going through the alphabet while picturing the face or object I'm trying to name still works sometimes. However, that method is time-consuming. Coming up with mnemonics is a speedier way of recalling the word I want. Give it a try if you are experiencing what I described.

It's important to repeat that I don't write down every single word I attempted to say and couldn't say if the word wasn't that important to me. However, I doubt that situation happens more than once-a-month. No big deal to me.

And consider this: If I can begin a book that will soon be completed, I am proving to myself that I still "have it." You can have it, too.

MORE ON MEMORY AND COMMUNICATION

Consider the difference between the memory of a one year old child and an 80 year old Alzheimer's patient. For the one-year old, he has gone through what I think of as four stages of development. For the 80 year old with Alzheimer's, she or he has also gone through those same stages. However, the order in which those stages occur are reversed. This order gives us a better understanding of memory over time.

Notice or See   Acknowledge   Recognize   Identify or Name

Great-grandson Jackson celebrated his first birthday last week. As a tiny baby, he noticed people; he saw them. After a few months, he acknowledged familiar others with a smile. A few months later, he began to recognize certain people. Finally, at a year old, Jackson now names several people – Mama, Dadda, PopPop, The first three stages are nonverbal. Only the final one is verbal. Jackson's brain is thriving.

The 80 year old Alzheimer's patient no longer identifies or names people. She does not recognize people. She only sometimes acknowledges people around her. She rarely notices or sees others.

The one-year old moved swiftly through all four memory stages while the 80 year old with Alzheimer's gradually slipped backwards through the same memory stages until she reached the final stage. Her brain is dying and her memory along with it.

Why include memory and communication in a book whose heart and soul is human behavior? I'm not sure it makes sense to others, although it makes sense to me. It seems to me that our youngest and our oldest are most at-risk for abuse from those within the family and those outside the family. Today, the term Family does not necessarily mean or include both biological parents. It also can be a revolving series of non-biological parents who find children a nuisance – an invasion into their private adult life. Many turn to misbehavior in one form or another. Too many revolving, non-biological "parents," tend to move in and move out of children's lives, leaving little positive imprint on the child's memory. Too many leave a negative imprint. A practice of using physical force to "punish" the natural and developmental behavior of young children is one frequent headline in today's newspapers and on the internet, as well. Children who are in the way of the self-centered lifestyle of the current "Daddy" or "Mommy" are at high risk of physical and psychological injury – or worse.

Let's just eliminate the "socially correct" watered-down, be careful of offending someone approach to the truth. Who is protecting our at-risk children from daily abuse by a non-biological "parent?" Or, sad but true, the child being abused by one of his biological parents? It's not that uncommon.

Likewise, the more we all understand the behavior of older folks who are experiencing diminishing brain function, yet appear to be misbehaving instead, the more caring and patient we will be. Dementia and Alzheimer's victims are not misbehaving and must not be physically or psychologically "punished."

It's certainly more pleasant to learn about the beauty of a developing child than it is to learn about the dimming of that long-ago bright light. No matter the age of the reader, consider that the dimming of light will come to you if you live long enough.

Adler, Dreikurs and Ansbacher described the caring for others in our lives. They called it "social interest." That means we are called upon to be as much interested in others as we are interested in ourselves. These three men believed all human beings had three life tasks: love, work and friendship. How are we doing with those tasks?

FAMILY DYNAMICS AND BIRTH ORDER

The word for the letter **I** was Influence. Consider how we are influenced by our parents, our brothers and sisters – even our aunts, uncles, cousins, grandparents and step-parents. Altogether, those relatives have the potential to influence us in good ways and not-so-good ways. We might say we are influenced by many of them, although it tends to be more like one or two who truly influence us in significant ways. As children, we probably move in the direction of those whose influence we want. That makes sense. For example, my parents had just two children. My brother is 8 years older than me. I consider him very influential in my life. We may also reject those whose influence we don't want – probably because we don't want to be like them. All of these things and more make up Family Dynamics because they include more people than just those who lived in your house as you were growing up. Relatives tend to live other places yet they can influence us no matter where we grew up or live now. Here's another possibility to consider. We can be influenced by words written by our favorite authors during our childhood – and beyond. Teenagers and those in their 20's can be greatly influenced by social "movements" and their leaders during their young adulthood. For now, however, it would take another book just to describe and document the concept of Family Dynamics. Adler and Ansbacher were a significant influence on the concept of family dynamics and birth order. Their works would be helpful for further exploration.

From this concept of Family Dynamics, we're going to pull out a segment of it called Birth Order. Teachers, parents and women of all ages seem to really enjoy our explorations of Birth Order, especially their own order of birth and what it tends to mean for them. When we explore Birth Order in a group setting, there are rules to accept and follow. Should a group member be unable to accept or follow those rules, they may not participate. All must agree beforehand that they will respect the privacy of those who volunteer to explore their own birth order. Over years of offering Birth Order in courses and workshops, everyone followed the rules.

Exploring Birth Order in a group setting can be revealing, full of surprises and, sometimes, emotional. Often, some bits of knowledge coming out are clarifying. Some negative thoughts about a sibling carried around for years by an individual may prove to have been faulty thinking. Sometimes I would ask group members who were teachers to write down the first name of the student who gives them the most trouble with misbehavior. FIRST-NAME ONLY – or just an initial. I wanted to help them discover whether or not that student resembled a brother or sister – or cousin. A few would say, "yes" and then we would look at the birth order of those who said, "yes" and discover something important. The behavior of that sibling – even physical description – tended to be like the misbehaving student. The question I had to ask was: *Could it be that when you look at that student, you see and hear your sister?* Sometimes the nonverbal response needed no words. Other times, responses were, "Oh, yes!" or "I hope not – I wouldn't want another person to be like my sister," or "I'm not sure. I need time to digest this." No one is ever pressured to participate in a full-blown exploration. Volunteers only. What seemed amazing, however, is how many teachers confessed their worst-behaved students reminded them of a brother or sister or neighbor they didn't get along with. Whenever teachers confessed to this discovery, I would ask them to repeat this statement. *Delilah is not my sister* **or** *Dennis is not my brother.* Then I asked them to repeat it.

Those teachers who confessed were asked to go back to school tomorrow and look at Delilah or Dennis through a different lens. They were to give more positive attention to that student and come back to report on what happened. More often than not, the misbehavior diminished although a perfect student did not suddenly emerge. What did emerge, however, was the teacher's realization that she or he was using faulty logic by transferring negative sibling traits to a student. The teacher became the learner and that's always a good thing. In a few instances, the teacher promised to "bury the hatchet" with that sibling, now an adult.

All of the above is offered as a preview or overview to actual Birth Order explorations by friends, colleagues and parents. After we look at a few different explorations, we'll offer more clarification. The only changes I'll make are to give all participants different names. All are from individuals who volunteered to explore the family in which they grew up and discuss birth order and their place in the family. They gave me the OK to include them in the book.

The following will help clarify all of the above. I believe that in order for every adult who feels dissatisfied with daily life or confused by conflict between and among adult siblings could be enlightened. By enlightened, I mean taking an extensive look at their place in the family in which they grew up. How did they fit? Who influenced them the most? In what way? Who made them happy? Was there competition or conflict somewhere within the family unit?

There are dozens of questions that can be answered by an exploration of your Birth Order. Within an hour, you can learn a great deal about yourself as well as the others who lived with you while growing up.

The following is important.

Ages of parents can matter. Years between parents can be important. Years between siblings matter a lot. Gender can matter a lot. A mother's miscarriage can matter and, if known, included in the order of birth. The death of a child at birth or in childhood can be very important to know. If the child's name is known, it is written and circled to indicate the child is not living. If the name is not known, draw a halo in the correct order of birth. In a way, a child who died wears a "halo" and will always be the family "angel." Angels never misbehave. The living siblings, however, can and do! Some parents carry the silent pain of that child's death throughout their other children's growing years

Step-parents need to be included, if they were in your house a significant amount of time as you were growing up. If grandparents lived in your house while you were growing up, they need to be included in your birth order exploration. How did they influence you?

The 2 or 3 traits for each family member are given by the person participating in the exploration. Exception is that the individual participating cannot suggest her own traits. Most of the time in these sessions, a friend, spouse or colleague will identify 2 or 3 traits for that person.

My birth order chart would show that I am 8 years younger than Jimmy, my brother. That means he is an "only" as well as the first born. That also means I am an "only" and the "baby." Jimmy was always my big brother. His influence as an outstanding softball pitcher found his baby sister becoming a softball pitcher, as well. Everything I know about the Phillies I learned from him. Today, although we are older adults, I'm still the baby. Once the baby, always the baby. My brother and I remain close to each other even though almost 3,000 miles separate us. Jimmy's wife – my sister-in-law, Nancy, was an only child. Her influences couldn't come from siblings.

Birth order is so very important for people to understand, especially when there is misbehavior as adults. By misbehavior, I mean alienation, anger, jealousy, arguments and family reunions "ruined" by words best left unspoken. The family unit is everything to us during our childhood and it remains everything to us as we grow older. Cherish it.

BIRTH ORDER EXPLORATION #1

Dad is 5 years older than Mom
Mom

Sarah is first born
Marsha is 2 years younger than Sarah
Mike is 5 years younger than Marsha

7 YEARS BETWEEN FIRST BORN AND LAST BORN

Sarah is a teacher participating in a Birth Order exploration. Her co-worker chose these traits: born leader, musical, caring
Sarah gave her sister, Marsha, these traits: athletic, ditzy, pretty
Sarah gave her brother, Mike, these traits: spoiled, handsome, irresponsible

Sarah gave these traits to her father: old-fashioned, quiet, intelligent
Sarah gave these traits to her mother: pretty, permissive parent, outgoing

As Sarah talked about her birth order, she realized as first-born, she was "strict" with her sister, Marsha – critical of Marsha's energy and obsession with looking in a mirror (all the time!) With Mike, Sarah felt the "baby" and only boy got extra-attention from their mother and Marsha – and that he was very spoiled and got away with misbehavior she could never have gotten away with. As an adult, Mike plays in a band, although he doesn't play the kind of music Sarah likes, so she seldom attends one of his "gigs." Sarah tended to feel she was the only serious, self-disciplined one of the children – she identified with her Dad and felt she was more like him than anyone else in the family. She also believed Marsha was a "clone" of their mother and both spent too much money on clothes. It irritated Sarah that Marsha would never accept Sarah's "hand-me down" clothing and their parents never insisted she do so. Sarah felt her Dad's only negative trait was that he was too generous.

Much more came out of Sarah's exploration although the high points were, as written. The group in Sarah's session felt Sarah was a born teacher and leader and that teachers and leaders tend to be first-born, although not always.

BIRTH ORDER EXPLORATION #2

Dad
Mom is same age as Dad

Diane is first born
Skipper is 4 ½ years younger than Diane
Jen is 7 years younger than Skipper

11 ½ YEARS BETWEEN FIRST AND LAST BORN CHILD

Diane is a school administrator participating in a Birth Order exploration. Her husband chose these traits: intelligent, responsible, stubborn

Diane gave her brother these traits: brilliant, Asberger- like, interesting

Diane gave her sister these traits: poor decision-maker, kind, animal lover

Diane gave her Dad these traits: intelligent, kind, funny
Diane gave her Mom these traits: caring, tenacious, smart

Diane is a school administrator. She was 4 ½ when her brother was born and 11 ½ years old when her sister was born. Those years in-between change things. Diane was the first-born and almost 5 years old when Skipper was born. That age spread suggests Diane was not just a first born but an "only" for almost 5 years. Diane likely has traits of leadership as well as the ability to function well on her own as an "only." She is comfortable with older people. She received her parents' undivided attention. Her brother offered her little or no competition as, although she sees him as brilliant, he also has issues that challenge him. Jen is a different person from her sister and brother. She was born 7 years after Skipper and 11 ½ years after Diane. Jen is not only the "baby" – she is also an "only." Her parents were older when she was born and may not have had the energy or determination to insist their "baby" be an achiever like her older siblings. Dianne, as almost a teenager when Jen was born, may have been a hard act to follow and Skipper may have been too "different" in personality to interest her, except in a more clinical way – such as, wondering how he became brilliant as well as "different." With animals, Jen could shine in her own way. She may not have had the pressure of expectations to be the academic success story her siblings were. She might be more laid back and let life flow however it wants.

Getting back to Diane is personally interesting to me. As a friend, I see in her something I've rarely seen before. I see Diane as being influenced almost equally by both parents. She had them to herself for almost 5 years – she inherited (or chose) their traits – all of them! Intelligent, kind, funny, caring, tenacious and smart. She is an amazing individual and her determination is such that when she comes up with a brilliant project, step out of her way while she is "on the move." She completes everything she begins. It is clear how strongly Diane was influenced by both mother and father.

I found it interesting that Diane considered her father "intelligent" and her mother "smart." There is a difference in those labels yet they are often used interchangeably. Diane likely had a good reason for the differentiation. Had Diane's father not had those soft traits of "kind" and "funny," he might have had challenges with his wife's "tenacious and smart" traits. Diane's mother's "caring" ways provided a soft trait to help balance things in her parent's marriage.

As for her husband's choice of "stubborn" for a trait for Diane, we could substitute "tenacious" which was a trait Diane gave for her mother. Most dictionaries define tenacious as "stubborn." People carefully choose words to identify traits – they do not haphazardly choose them. Many volunteers for this project silently mull over words in their mind before offering a description. Body language always speaks louder than spoken words. And so, I believe Diane intended to use tenacious for her mother. While Diane's husband offered "stubborn" as a trait for his wife, he could have suggested the word "determined." Funny how people who know or knew each other well can come up with several words for a trait that means almost the same thing.

BIRTH ORDER EXPLORATION #3

Mom is 3 yrs. Older than Dad
Dad

Shawn is first born
Gina is 3 years younger than Shawn
Deanne is 1 year younger than Gina
Trevor is 5 years younger than Deanne

9 YEARS BETWEEN FIRST AND LAST BORN CHILD

Gina is a counselor participating in a Birth Order exploration. Her husband and a friend chose these traits: resourceful, sensitive, a listener.

Gina gave Shawn these traits: insecure, loyal, sense of humor.

Gina gave Deanne these traits: opinionated, family-oriented, talkative.

Gina gave Trevor these traits: athletic, irresponsible, self-centered.

Looking at Gina's birth order position tells us she was 6 years old when Trevor was born and Deanne was just 5 years old. The closeness in age of the girls in the family tends to go in two directions – either they were close growing up or were competitive with one another. My impression is that they were competitive since Deanne was opinionated and talkative and Gina's traits are quite different. Both girls can be considered a "middle child." Yet, Gina's traits seem more suited to becoming a counselor than Deanne's. It's unusual to discover opinionated, talkative individuals as successful counselors. They need to be listeners, as is Gina. A friend who knows Gina offers additional traits that can be significant to her role as a highly successful counselor. She is seen as intelligent and also modest. Gina does not seek the limelight that she could have had. She yields the limelight to others and is happy for their success. Like her mother, she is a hard-worker, self-reliant, self-less and dedicated to her role as counselor and friend.

Gina's parents did not have a long marriage due to her Dad's death at age 36. He died of a heart attack. Her mother was 39 at the time of her Dad's death. Trevor, the youngest child and second son, had less time with both parents than did the older three siblings. In birth order, Trevor had two birth order positions – youngest as well as only. Five years or more between siblings suggests Trevor is influenced by both positions. As for Trevor being athletic like his Dad who died young, he may or may not have been influenced by stories about his Dad's athleticism. Often, the youngest in a family is the athletic one even when the father is not. The youngest in a family is also often seen as the "spoiled/self-centered" and "irresponsible" sibling – the one who didn't have to follow the family rules the older ones were required to follow.

Trevor, as the baby as well as the only, was likely more drawn to Gina's sensitivity and resourcefulness than Deanne's opinionated, talkative traits. On the other hand, Deanne appears to be the sibling who is more family-oriented and could fit as Trevor's other mother. It's fascinating to learn how often a youngest child – a male – realizes he had several "mothers" when his sisters were older than he.

Shawn, the first born, is seen as insecure. That is not a typical trait for a first born son. He had both parents all to himself for 3 years – very formative years. Both parents seem like good role models without being harsh disciplinarians or parents who pressure-groom their first son to be a leader. Shawn's loyalty and sense of humor may have compensated for his lack of leadership qualities. Also, Shawn may have been the sibling who missed his father the most when his Dad died at age 36 and Shawn was just 10 years old. I feel bad myself just thinking how hard it was for Gina's mother, Shawn and Deanne to cope without a Dad. And Trevor was just 2 when his dad died – too young to really know him. He likely was "babied" by his sisters, along with his widowed mother. After I proposed this possibility to Gina, she laughed and said it was true. Here are her words: "Yes. My sister and I even called him Baby. Our mother also referred to him as "Baby." Is it a surprise to anyone that two of Trevor's traits are *irresponsible* and *self-centered*?

Gina grew up in a family where there was early happiness and "intactness" that was disrupted much too soon by her father's death. Her mother's strength and coping ability certainly helped her to regroup as a family unit without a husband and father who brought fun and laughter to his family. Gina's one description of the father she remembers was that "He liked a good time."

BIRTH ORDER EXPLORATION #4

Dad
Mom is 2 years younger than Dad

Blake is first born
Celeste is 2 years younger than Blake

2 YEARS BETWEEN FIRST AND SECOND CHILD

Celeste is a school administrator participating in a Birth Order exploration. She holds a Doctorate Degree in Education. She is a Language Arts Specialist. Her husband chose these traits: conscientious, gentle, generous and perfectionistic.

Celeste gave her older brother, Blake, these traits: driven, focused and organized.

Celeste gave her Dad these traits: responsible, capable, perfectionistic and principled.

Celeste gave her Mom these traits: conscientious, gracious, gentle, sage.

Celeste is two years younger than her brother, Blake. With just two children in the family, we cannot name a middle child. We also cannot name an only child. Since she was born just two years after her brother, it will be difficult to see Celeste as "the baby" in the family.

Blake is the first born and only son. His traits are similar to most first-born sons of parents who value education and high performance in their career choice. That Blake is "driven" could be both blessing and burden. His other traits of "focused and organized" also suggest they would bring this person business success without a sense of peace or contentment since he might be driven to keep moving to the next level. Would he ever reach a level which could bring him peace and a measure of happiness and contentment? Only Blake could tell us the answer.

Blake indicates a close alignment with his father's traits. Blake and his Dad seem to have been success stories in some sort of business or corporation. They were or still are high achievers. Where Blake and his Dad may differ is that the son is "driven" and the Dad doesn't seem to have that trait. That makes the Dad sound "softer" in personality.

Celeste, as a high achiever, seems to have the traits of both parents. She gets her soft side from her mother - traits of being gentle and conscientious as well as traits that suggest caring and giving ways. However, Celeste and her Dad both are perfectionists, one of the most difficult traits to master and still find happiness. Yet those who know Celeste well know her to be a happy, cheerful person who lights up a room when she enters it. It appears that both parents were highly influential in Celeste's childhood years.

Celeste's use of the term "sage" is fascinating. That term is almost synonymous with "wise," yet Celeste did not choose that term to describe her mother's trait. Celeste's choice suggests that her mother was beyond "wise" – if that is possible!

Blake was not given the trait of perfectionist, although he seems to come close to it. Could it be he was a perfection-*seeker* yet felt he never measured up to his Dad's and sister's achievement? As for Blake being "driven," that trait could be more exhausting to an individual than the trait of perfectionist.

Celeste's birth order and family dynamics suggest all family members achieved at high levels of thinking yet both parents seemed to balance out the cerebral with the sensitive, which has to be difficult to accomplish. Celeste's leadership was responsible for the literacy success of our school district's success. She is the warmest and kindest perfectionist I know.

BIRTH ORDER EXPLORATION #5

Mom is 6 months older than Dad
Dad

Two miscarriages
Stillborn-full-term Baby Boy
Sybil
Suzette
Kit
Stuart
Miscarriage

9 YEARS BETWEEN FIRST AND LAST BORN CHILD

Sybil is a school administrator participating in a Birth Order exploration. Her friends chose these traits for her: high energy, creative, tall.

Sybil disclosed that her parents' first child was a stillborn baby boy.

Sybil was born 2 years later, as the first born and the second born

Sybil gave Suzette these traits: creative, determined, highly accomplished.

Sybil gave Kit these traits: entertainer, "nervy," fragile.

Sybil gave Stuart these traits: worker, recovering alcoholic, loyal

Sybil gave her father these traits: romantic, active, handsome, man's man

Sybil gave her mother these traits: great mom, organized, good listener

Sybil's participation verified her creativity. Creative she is! Sybil offered not only the birth order of the childhood family she grew up in but also the birth order of her daughters and grandchildren. For today, however, let's concentrate on her childhood family, which seems like a good family in which to grow up. Sybil functions well as a first born. She believes her parents raised her as a first born, even though two miscarriages and a full-term stillborn baby were their first babies. We wonder what it was like for them to have three daughters in a row before Stuart arrived as their only living son and youngest child. He was likely special to his parents and, perhaps, his sisters who had no early knowledge of a miscarriages and a stillborn brother.

Sybil is unique in her role as a school administrator in that the highly creative side of her is not common among school administrators. Unusual projects emerge with her school staff and the use of vivid colors "paint" the walls. Her physical and mental energy seem endless. To know Sybil is to sense she has always lived the life of a person who relishes change, travel and new experiences. She seems to be a "Born Free" individual with virtually no fears. Her courage is to be admired.

Suzette doesn't seem to be in conflict with her high energy, creative older sister. Their traits are similar and may have offered them a close relationship without undue competition. However, early on in life, Sybil and Suzette were not close. It took adulthood for them to become closer.

Two years after Suzette's birth, Kit arrived. Kit's traits, according to Sybil, include "nervy" and "fragile." Those traits also suggest issues that may separate her from her older sisters, at least in strength and determination. The term fragile would not apply to either Sybil or Suzette. Rather, fragile suggests a weakness while the term "nervy" suggests Kit is willing to take chances that others might not take. Still, Kit worked as a therapist for people with eating disorders. There could be challenges to Kit that her older sisters appeared not to have. Three years after Kit's birth, Stuart was born. A brother's birth was likely a happy event for the whole family. As the baby, Stuart may have been "babied" by his three sisters as well as his parents. His place in the family was quite unique. As time went on, perhaps Stuart felt overwhelmed by his three older talented, creative, accomplished sisters. One of his traits is "a worker," which suggests he went in a different direction from his sisters – in a direction that wasn't, perhaps, as zesty as the girls'? Did he ever attempt to walk in his sisters' footprints? Did he ever show any special talent in the area of creativity or entertaining? He is seen as "loyal" which suggests he had strong feelings and ties to his family. When did he first want or need alcohol? As a teenager, or later in his life? That remains an open question.

The three sisters seemed to have little or no competition with one another. All three were beautiful and talented from childhood – and throughout their adulthood. They seemed to relish each other's accomplishments. Kit passed away in 2016. Her sisters were devastated at their loss. Although Sybil and Suzette were closer, their love and admiration for Kit was genuine. Kit's death broke a bond that was rare. It is unusual for three sisters to grow up without undue competition with one another.

Look at the parents of the daughters and son who lived. We can't know how the parents reacted to the birth of a son after having lost their first one. Only 7 years separate Sybil from Stuart. Four siblings (now three) appeared to have had a childhood filled with enchantment. For Sybil to consider her Dad "romantic, active and handsome," suggests an almost Fairy Tale life. For Sybil to consider her Mother a "great mom, organized and a good listener" suggests a happy blending of the parents' traits. One had to be the steady hand with handling the reality of parenting with the fun and magic of Dad's charm and entertainment. The parents seemed to balance their marriage well.

Sybil provided me with additional information about her family. Her mother had another miscarriage after Stuart's birth. The earlier miscarriages were attributed to the 10,000 ft. altitude in Peru. The stillbirth of the baby which preceded Sybil's birth was attributed to mother's bout with German Measles.

Before Sybil was born, her parents lived in Lima, Peru where her Dad was a mining engineer. He and Sybil's mother wanted children. When it appeared they would have difficulty giving birth to full-term healthy babies, they moved to the west coast of the United States and the healthy babies began to arrive. Sybil truly was their first born and in her adulthood, it is no surprise that she knows how to take charge and lead.

In my years of studying and making birth order charts with volunteers, I never cease to be amazed how our behavior is shaped within the family. It has been a privilege to share family birth order and character traits with others. As for the family in which Sybil grew up, hers may be the most unique I've come upon. At the end of our exploration, Sybil dropped another surprise! When her Dad was in his 60's, he took a mining job in El Salvador. Since her mother was caretaker for her own aging parents, she chose not to go. And so, her Dad went alone. It seems he wasn't alone for long. He and his 20-year old housekeeper had a "love child." Eventually, the family got to meet them.

Sybil said I may share this part of her birth order exploration for the book. I'm so glad she did. Fascinating – just like Sybil.

THE JOURNEY PROGRAM

U pper Elementary classroom teachers were finding each new school year more stressful due to an increase in misbehavior. More and more kids misbehaved on the school bus, in the classroom, in the cafeteria, in the hallway and on the playground - and the teachers had to be involved in their discipline.

Each summer, we had meaningful grade level inservice days where gripes were vented, Needs and Wants lists were agreed upon, report card revisions were made and bagels and fresh fruit were consumed. (note: since I retired, no refreshments are served. I consider that to be misbehavior on the part of school leaders). Most of the gripes each summer were about kids whose misbehavior was just unacceptable. Teachers agreed that if just one or two major misbehavin' students were removed from their classroom, the behavior of the rest of the kids would be manageable.

After not having any luck with ideas and recommendations to the School Board for hiring teacher aides, we were almost ready to give up. Finally, we came up with a concept that would eventually be approved. Here's what we presented to the Board of Education for approval.

Develop a six-week program for about 10-12 identified 4th, 5th or 6th graders who are seriously disruptive to the smooth flow in their classroom. After six weeks are completed, students will be returned to their classroom in the belief that their behavior will be improved and they will "fit in" better than before their Journey experience. The Journey classroom will operate away from the regular classrooms of the Journey students. It is important that Journey students experience a kind of Time Away from the social group to which they belong by assignment. Six weeks in Journey is not punishment. Instead, it is a chance for Journey students to understand that their intelligence and creativity can work *for* them instead of *against* them – that their misbehavior was gaining them nothing positive. Journey will benefit these students by encouraging them to use their gifts to lead as well as to follow – to listen to ideas of their teacher and classmates and to respect others. Students will also have solid average to above average intelligence as well as demonstrate creative thinking or a special talent. The grade-level curriculum in math, science and language arts will follow students to the Journey classroom and will be explored for most of the morning session. The afternoon session will find each student engaged in a unique project – determined by the student and approved by the Journey teacher. Materials will be supplied through donations from parents, the school art teacher and left-overs from classroom teachers happy to get rid of excess "stuff."

All of the above planning and dreaming was taking place the year before Journey was launched. Since each Journey student would spend six weeks in the program, we could actually select several groups of 10-12 throughout the school year at any given time. You can be assured that no one Journey group would be exactly like another. Each group would have its own personality, challenges and ideas. Within a 180 day required school year attendance, several Journey groups would be created – so that approximately 50 students could experience the Journey Program in each school year. The Journey teacher would need two days between groups in order to create a new setting and prepare to greet 10 -12 newcomers.

The teacher we approached to become our Journey teacher was the easiest part of our launch. A very special kind of teacher was required – one who was very bright, tolerant, patient, creative and gifted in her own right – and one who proved able to handle the 4th, 5th and 6th grade math, science and language arts lessons along with creative and unique afternoon projects. That teacher would be handling parent contacts, as well. A teacher aide would be hired for 25 hours a week and the teacher would be the one to select and supervise that aide. Mrs. C joyfully agreed to the challenge of being our Journey teacher. She was a teacher in our upper elementary Gifted Program. To our way of thinking, Journey students needed a teacher who was, in her own right, gifted. Mrs. C was the perfect choice. She was the catalyst for the success of our Journey students as they returned to their assigned classroom. She maintained brief correspondence with each former student, on occasion – not too often and not too seldom. After all, the goal was to return former Journey students to their more permanent social group – where they had become a better fit socially and emotionally. In other words, better-behaved and more self-disciplined kids who can "make it" in their assigned class setting and not just in a Journey setting.

How were students chosen for Journey? Our district's 4th, 5th and 6th grade level population ranged from 275 to 300 students per grade level. Classroom teachers gave the building principals the names of students recommended. We asked the teachers to limit recommendations to two. Principals would submit names to me and, together, after hours of discussion, we would agree to 10, (eventually up to 12). Parents were then called and met with their child's principal who described the Journey Program and its expected benefits to their child. As you may have guessed, more boys than girls were recommended for Journey. Ratio tended to be eight boys to two girls. Parents of the recommended students were not surprised. They already knew their kids were disruptive and discipline challenges from kindergarten on. It was rare for us to have to coax a parent into signing the agreement we developed to keep things official. When parents discovered the Journey teacher was a teacher of gifted students, their eyes lit up and you could see the positive effect it had on them. More than one parent said, "Finally! Someone else besides me believes my kid is really bright and not just a pain in the butt."

The classroom teachers who had a student in Journey provided Mrs. C with a week's worth of math, science and language arts lessons, worksheets and activities, as well as texts and other essential supplies, so that when Journey students returned to the classroom, they would be on target with that population. Afternoon projects tended to be unique, challenging and of high personal interest to the student. Most projects were "hands-on." Only rarely did a student choose an academic theme paper that required extensive research. Projects could last as short as a week – which meant five more projects would have to be chosen – or as long as two weeks. At two weeks, students would have to choose three projects. At the end of a student's six weeks in Journey, he or she would return to the regular classroom. Informal kinds of behavior lessons were sprinkled throughout the day by Mrs. C and her aide. There was a big emphasis on the importance of returning to their regular classrooms "more mature," better-behaved and respectful of others.

After a big "hello" to curious classmates, the returning Journey student would make a brief presentation in front of the class, describing the Journey experience and, perhaps, sharing a finished project or two. Projects ranged from a house and barn made of popsicle sticks and tooth-picks and painted creatively to several paper mache' dinosaurs that included research on each kind, to some incredible paintings in frames made by the students. Several sculptures were created that drew a lot of attention from the art teacher. Thanks to several parent volunteers, some students learned to crochet. Mrs. C brought some influential and interesting guests to visit and chat with the Journey kids. Examples of visitors were a retired Army General, an author of children's books and a carpenter. These visitors were special to the students and each one provided a positive influence on the kids. Our goal for Journey students was to return to the regular classrooms more self-disciplined and with a more mature way of looking at the school experience to which he or she was returning and belonging. On my own last day of school, the Journey students gave me a large wooden Butterfly Box for my home garden. They all had a hand in creating it. Priceless.

We've just skimmed the basic information about our Journey

Program in order to encourage public educators to move away from that "one size fits all curriculum." In far to many schools, the old, worn-out, irrelevant curriculum is like feeding all students a bagel that has sat out, uncovered, for 10 days and then eaten without any cream cheese.

THERE IS NO END TO MISBEHAVIN' - YET

My deep, deep belief as a mother, grandmother, public school educator, school administrator, author and consultant, is this. Ever since the mostly appropriate school curriculum of the 1950's ended – and with the scientific advances of the Russians that led them to success with Sputnik – public schools in the United States aimed high while falling low and on a downward spiral. It was impressive, this rush to beat the Russians at their own scientific game. The general public, of course, didn't know the inevitable unwanted consequences at the time. Neither did the brilliant scientists and mathematicians who were in charge of rapid change in public schooling. The politicians probably didn't know it, either, although they thought if the smartest people in the country believed it, they would want a piece of the action. As politicians tend to – they got on a bandwagon that was bound to excite the voters. Little did they know they were about to make a big mess out of the school curriculum, teaching-learning practices and increased misbehavior in students, a mess that survives to this day.

I wrote my first book, based that historic moment with Sputnik, and called it *Curriculum Gone Astray: When Push Came to Shove*. The curriculum gone astray brought with it an academic nightmare of inappropriate grade level expectations and goals when the intention was to do just the opposite. In addition to developmentally inappropriate, yet required standardized testing at the elementary level, the nightmare intensified. Unwritten class and school rules, paired with punishment instead of logical consequences for each rule broken, prevailed. Not enough teacher support, not enough parental partnership, too much emphasis on computer use and not enough on trust-building, face-to-face relationship building and character development, created the mess we're in now.

At home and within the family, the same can be said for the lack of no-nonsense rules applied consistently, along with logical consequences, character development and trust-building. Add to these are seemingly unlimited use of Iphones and computers. Phones and computers and other electronics have their place in our homes and in our lives. However, what are the negative effects of the almost addictive quality they produce? Parents have a right to occasionally monitor where their children are visiting on their computers. It might be best not to do this in secret but with their kids standing by. This builds trust, over time, between kids and parents. If parents do their inherited jobs as parents, they will be sending their children to school more self-disciplined, more balanced, more caring of others and happier. They will see school as a place where they belong to a different kind of caring family and will be more eager and serious about learning new things.

At work, at a place of worship, in the military, or retired and "living the life," we need to feel we belong, to know others care about our well-being, to believe we can trust the next two generations that come along to be well-educated, caring, trustworthy, of good character and less misbehaving than those who preceded them.

My point of view is that public school teachers and administrators across the country believe public education needs a major overhaul – a kind of rebirth. I've come to the conclusion that our beloved United States of America, led by leaders elected by us, has already given unplanned birth to at least two generations of a permissive, Me First, no-rules, no consequences and abuse of our First Amendment rights. Add to that, unplanned birth, spectacular entertainment needs, addiction to electronics as well as to illegal and prescription drugs, maxed out credit cards, fractured family lives - and to top it off - a "poor manners with no empathy for others" style of living.

May our country, with its freedoms, natural beauty and resources as well as opportunities, never reach THE END. I know too many individuals who are doing great work with children and too many parents of young children who are doing everything right for their kids. My negative comments, however, do not come out easily from my thoughts, which is why I have surprised myself at my worry about the future that awaits all of us. Do I feel this way because I am an old fogey? Do I really believe our society is in as much trouble as I think it is? My answer is: sometimes yes, sometimes, no.

This country may have just one more generation *to begin* to undo the damage done over the past 60 years – to our children, our education system, our families, our old folks, our politics, our neglect of mental health issues, our messed up health care system, our elected officials, our Constitution, our laws, our transportation system, our reckless driving, along with road rage, and finally, our basic human kindness, all that seem to have become as "at risk" as our youngest children.

If I offended anyone, I hope I only offended the ones who have taken misbehavior to an intolerable level. If, like my family, friends and colleagues, the reader does not belong in a category just described, you know who you are. Keep on keeping on!

Give me a little writing space to pick on professional sports. I love professional baseball and professional basketball, although I especially love college basketball and March Madness. Professional football is sometimes OK.

Let's begin with the MLB, followed by the NBA and the NFL. Professional baseball players, raging in revenge, who use their bats and helmets to pummel trash cans, boxes of sunflower seeds and juice barrels to oblivion are a bad influence on our children. Baseball pitchers who throw at the heads and bodies of opposition batters, are a bad influence on our children. Same goes for the NBA players who attempt to gain power and control over their opposition by blatant tripping and choking and shoving. Double Ditto for NFL players whose immature behavior on and off the field are unnecessary for winning games. What kind of influence do the immature players and their misbehavior have on kids? The majority of professional athletes are good role models for the kids who idolize them. Too bad those few serious misbehavin' players are allowed to escape the consequences due to their exceptional athletic ability.

Who is in charge these days? Where are the leaders? Come on, people! Let's make things better.

I am a life-long sports nut as well as a professional sports critic where misbehavior is concerned. If we begin to require better behavior from our athletes and their coaches, reduce the number of F-words spoken/bleeped in interviews, perhaps kids in school will get the message and clean up their own kinds of misbehavior. Too much to ask? I don't think so.

We need a joint effort with common goals – the marriage of home, school and the community-at-large in more than just words. And we have to begin with parents of the baby in the cradle and the toddler on the trike and then make sure the pre-K and Kindergarten curriculum is appropriate to the sensory learner - a hands-on creature who needs more action and developmentally appropriate activity. It's the "doing" that will matter. As with everything else, the proof will be in the pudding.

Still, after all the negative behavior we encounter in our daily lives, the positive ones keep us hopeful, determined and in the pursuit of happiness. As for me, I love waking up every morning beside my husband of 59 years. I feel safe and happy and ready for another day of adventure. I am proud of the way my husband is battling his cancer and other health issues. He is brave and determined to either build another earth-berm-passive solar house or travel here, there and everywhere in some kind of trailer – with me, of course. Our bachelor son, Tod, left his law enforcement career in Virginia and North Carolina to move back to Pennsylvania to help out when his Dad's health issues began and his Mom also needed surgeries. Our married son, Ted, lives two hours away with his wife, Pam, who is like our second daughter. She is an RN, a happy Grandmother to Nathan and somebody special in all ways. Ted is a great cook, lover of cats and a proud grandfather to Nathan.

Ted and Tod are twins and such wonderful human beings. Ted makes us laugh and is the most social creature among us and Tod is the quieter, outdoorsman of our bunch. Tod also took on lots of his Dad's outdoor work and daily chores with farm animals when he returned "home" to us. He is selfless to the core.

Our daughter, Jill – our first-born child – is almost too unique to describe. She's always been beautiful yet that's not what we think of first when we think of Jill. We first think of her wanting to make sure everyone in the family is always connected – either by e-mail, Text, phone calls or visits. She helped to edit this manuscript and she was great at the task! If we could give her a different middle name, it would be Amazing Grace. She recently retired from 34 years of teaching 3rd graders – she was a master teacher. Jill is Grammy to Jackson. Her husband is Jackson's PopPop. Pure joy.

Jill's husband, Jerry, is like our 3rd son. Jerry recently retired from 35 years of teaching environmental science to Middle School students. He is always "there" for anyone in the family who needs him to help out in some way. He has also become quite an artist

Our very beautiful and talented granddaughter, Kristin, is our family's special sweetheart. Like her mother - our daughter, Jill - Kristin also makes sure we're all connected. Family means so much to her. Motherhood only perfected her, impossible as it may seem. She and her loving husband and golfer, Kyle, blessed us with our first great-grandchild, Jackson. This book is dedicated to Jackson. Uh oh. I said this would be the last book for me. We just found out that another great-grandchild will arrive in February of 2018. Looks like I'll have to write something to dedicate to that newest child. I can't favor one of life's blessings over another.

That would be misbehaving.

MY FAMILY